# Harry Frier's
# TAUNTON

M.H. JONES

*Somerset Books*

First published in 2002 by Somerset Books
Copyright © M.H. Jones 2002

British Library Cataloguing-in-Publication Data
A CIP record for this title is available from the British Library

ISBN 0 86183 461 5

SOMERSET BOOKS
*Official Publishers to Somerset County Council*
Halsgrove House
Lower Moor Way
Tiverton, Devon EX16 6SS
T: 01884 243242
F: 01884 243325
www.halsgrove.com

Printed in Hong Kong by Regal Printing Ltd

# Contents

*For Jan, with love.*

# A Note about the Illustrations

The illustrations are intended to be a representative sample of Harry Frier's output. They are arranged approximately in chronological order. It should be borne in mind, however, that the majority of illustrations and photographs are not referred to in the text. The selection and arrangement of the illustrations has been facilitated by Frier's practice of signing and dating his work in accordance with his own convention: a picture or drawing was usually signed and dated with the year of its completion and, if the preliminary sketch had been made some years before, that fact was occasionally stated on the finished picture as well. In cases where the subject depicted no longer existed, the date shown on Frier's drawing was that of the photograph or print from which he made the watercolour copy. As this practice was confusing he soon changed it and his drawings of such subjects were undated, and often unsigned, as were some of his commercial watercolours made at the end of his working life.

Dimensions of drawings illustrated and referred to in the text are those of the visible picture area, height before width. In most cases the area of picture reproduced in this book is slightly less than the whole picture: where the area reproduced is considerably less than that of the original, this is indicated by the word 'Detail' in the accompanying caption.

Many of the pictures illustrated belong either to the Somerset Archaeological and Natural History Society (SANHS) or to Taunton Deane Borough Council (TDBC). Individual owners of Frier pictures usually prefer to remain anonymous: such ownership is not indicated in the captions. Without the whole-hearted co-operation of these bodies and individuals the task of assembling the illustrations for this book could not have been undertaken. Although acknowledgement of other assistance received is made at the end of the book, it seems proper that the particular debt of gratitude to these bodies and individuals should be acknowledged here.

# *Prologue*

Towards the end of the First World War a topographical painter who had lived and worked in Somerset for almost forty years dropped from sight. His work was little known outside the town where he lived, and his death a few years later passed almost without notice. Most of his watercolour drawings have survived, and, perhaps because they represent a reaction against the artistic installations of today, are cherished as works of joyful simplicity, technical skill and some artistic merit.

More than eighty years after his death, therefore, it seemed worthwhile to find out and set down something of the life and work of this unknown. His name was Harry Frier, and although he lived for nearly forty years and died in Taunton, his life began more than seventy years earlier and five hundred miles to the north.

# The Frier Family

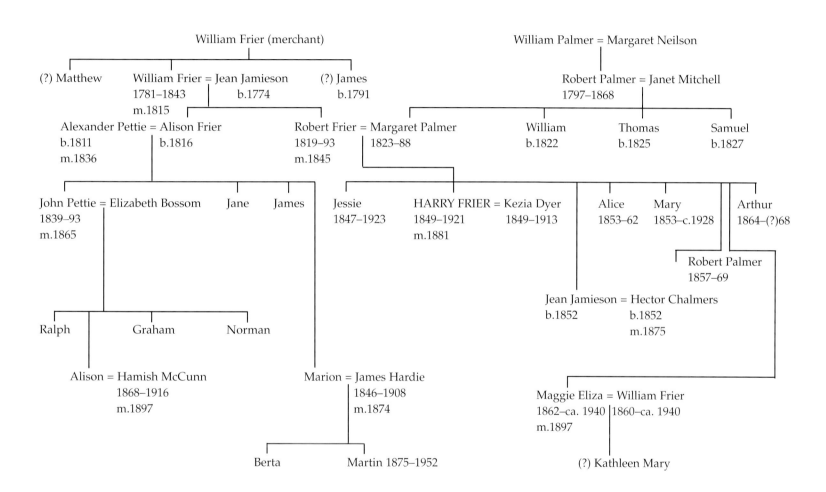

# Edinburgh

During the two centuries before 1815, Edinburgh had changed little. It had, it is true, encroached somewhat on the country to the south at the beginning of the eighteenth century and at the end of that century had acquired the satellite New Town to the north of the marshy ground by the Castle. Nevertheless, the Old Town, lying between the Castle on the west and the Palace of Holyrood House on the east, remained a maze of dark arches, stairs and alleys. The ways were so narrow that you could lay a hand on either wall, so steep that in the greasy winter weather, the pavement was almost as treacherous as ice. Washing dangled above washing from the windows, the houses bulged outwards on flimsy brackets, and, at the top of all, a gable and a few crowsteps were silhouetted against the sky.

In no other city did the sight of the country enter so far. You turned a corner and there was the sun going down into the Highland hills; you looked down an alley and saw ships tacking for the Baltic or coming into the port of Leith. From the quayside, waggons wound slowly up the hill to the warehouses of the merchants of the Old Town. By the early nineteenth century most of these merchants' premises were scarcely larger than small shops, and those engaged in similar trades often congregated in the same part of the city. This was an old tradition. In the Middle Ages, for example, the open space below the Castle had been frequented by the cloth merchants who set up their booths there. In the nineteenth century, cloth wholesalers occupied the same area in premises that were more permanent, but the medieval origin of their trade was perpetuated in the name of the street where they congregated, Lawnmarket.

A mile or so south of Lawnmarket was the shop of William Frier, master baker. In 1815 when he was in his early thirties, William married Jean Jamieson, seven years his senior. A year later, their daughter Alison was born, followed in 1819 by a son, Robert. Both children seem, in the manner of the Scots, to have been well educated. They grew up with a penchant for hard work and a deter-mination to raise themselves out of the artisan milieu into which they were born. In 1836, when she was twenty, Alison was married to Alexander Pettie, one of the Lawnmarket cloth merchants. Pettie had probably inherited the Lawnmarket business, but as the name had been common to several cloth traders in the area since 1800, we cannot be certain. When Alison's brother Robert Frier was in his early teens he was employed by Pettie in the business, first as a sales-man, and later as manager of the firm's retail premises at Currie, a village five miles south-west of the city. Within ten years, Robert Frier was Pettie's partner in the concern. In 1845 he married Margaret Palmer, daughter of the schoolmaster and parish clerk of Currie. Margaret was twenty-two and had been born at Colvend, then in Dumfriesshire.

By his marriage to a schoolmaster's daughter Robert Frier took the first step up the social ladder. They settled in Edinburgh, renting a house at Hope Park End near his father's bakery, at the south-east corner of the Meadows, a park on the site of a marshy lake known as the South Loch. Within four years Robert Frier resigned from the partnership and established his own drapery business in Lawnmarket. His business prospered, and by 1850 employed more than 100 hands. Robert and Margaret Frier's first child, Jessie, was born in 1847. Two years later the family moved to 5 Crichton Street in Edinburgh's Old Town, and it was here on Wednesday 2 May 1849 that their second child and eldest son, Harry Frier, was born. Although his forename was really Henry, and he is so referred to in all official documents, he was from his earliest age always known as Harry to his family and friends.

The Frier's third child, named Jean Jamieson after her paternal grandmother, was born in 1853. Later in the same year the impend-ing arrival of a fourth child necessitated a move to a larger house, and one in Ratcliff Place on the southern outskirts of the Old Town was selected. Here in 1854, not one, but two children were born, twin girls Alice Margaret and Mary. Robert Frier was now thirty-five years old; he had five young children and was owner of a prosperous drapery and clothing business. Although he was then considering diversifying into the manufacture of stockings, he was even at this time seriously contemplating a complete change of profession. In 1853 his first landscape painting had been accepted and hung in the annual exhibition of the Royal Scottish Academy, and it was the rapidity with which the cloth merchant's painting was sold in such august, if provincial, surroundings that perhaps prompted him to consider this radical change of occupation.

The rapidly increasing output of Scotland's long-established coal and iron industries, and its burgeoning chemical and shipbuilding trades meant that entrepreneurial profits had reached very high levels. This newly acquired wealth had gradually been disseminated through all levels of society so that by the middle of the nineteenth century even the lower classes enjoyed a standard of living higher than at any time in Scotland's history. For the first time they were earning more than was needed to buy the necessities of life. At the same time the connection of Edinburgh and Glasgow to London by rail in 1849 enabled thousands of Scots people to visit that vast storehouse of art and technology, the Great Exhibition of 1851. They became aware, perhaps for the first time, that they too could now buy objets d'art, the acquisition of which had until then been regarded as the prerogative of the aristocracy.

So it was that there was a great deal of indiscriminate buying, especially of pictures, by the middle classes, and this brought into being…

*a crowd of painters who had no real aptitude for art. The demand for pictures created the supply. Men who had been in business and had painted in an amateur way went in for art as a profession in much the same way as they would have gone into any other business opening; relaxing the old prejudice, parents sent their sons 'to be artists', as they might have apprenticed them to a trade or sent them to sell calico or tea. Some of these possessed the true feeling, but with more it was simply a pleasant and honourable calling, and save that they could find a market for their wares, there seemed no justification for their existence. (J L Caw Scottish Painting Past & Present, p. 227.)*

Although the paragraph quoted above records a general trend in Scottish art at this time, the motive that impelled Robert Frier to contemplate changing his career and joining this 'crowd of painters' remains a mystery. At a time when Scottish education was more advanced than that south of the border, most young people were

taught drawing and painting as part of their normal curriculum. If they showed promise, their artistic training was continued by drawing masters who visited the upper classes in their homes like piano tuners, or who received the sons and daughters of the middle classes in their studios for tuition in what was then regarded as merely a social accomplishment. The training usually took the form of copying the master's sketches in pencil and watercolour, and occasional sketching trips to nearby beauty spots in summer. Watercolour drawings were not usually acceptable for exhibition purposes at this time, so painters who wished to exhibit their works for sale at the annual exhibition of the Royal Scottish Academy, for example, were required to submit oil paintings. The change of technique was not difficult to accomplish.

*Robert Frier, father of Harry Frier. A carte-de-visite taken by an Edinburgh photographer.*

The training of professional artists, on the other hand, was the concern of an Academy that had been founded in 1760. An Act of Parliament of 1727 created the Honourable Board of Trustees for Manufactures in Scotland; to this board was given the proceeds of the sales of estates confiscated after the 1745 uprising, and some of the money used to found a school of design. At first this school, known as the Trustees' Academy, rented a room in Edinburgh University, but after several changes of premises and masters, found a permanent home in the building of the Royal Institution in Edinburgh. In 1852 the Trustees' Academy entered on its last and most famous period when Robert Scott Lauder became master. Born in 1803, the son of a tanner, Lauder had studied at the Trustees' Academy, after which he spent five years in Europe. From 1838–52 he worked in London where he gained a considerable reputation as a portrait painter, and when he was appointed master of the Trustees' Academy was considered to be one of the leading Scots artists of the day. In 1858, after a review of the function of the Board of

Manufactures, the Trustees' Academy was dismembered, the organisation of the life-drawing classes being taken over by the Royal Scottish Academy, which had been founded in 1826. The remainder of the classes were incorporated as the Edinburgh School of Art, with Lauder as its Principal until his retirement in 1861 following a paralytic stroke. The School's next years were not happy and it only regained something of the reputation of the former Trustees' Academy in the 1870s when responsibility for its running was handed over to the Scottish Education Department.

In the 1840s, courses at the Trustees' Academy were only held during the evenings, and as the Royal Institution building was at the northern end of the Mound, not far from Lawnmarket, it is tempting to suppose that Robert Frier may have studied painting at the Academy. Of the group of artists known to have been trained by Lauder at the Academy in the next decade, the most successful in his own lifetime was the historical painter, John Pettie, eldest son of Alexander Pettie, the Lawnmarket cloth merchant, and Alison Frier. John Pettie was born in 1839, and in 1852 his father sold the Lawnmarket business, and the family moved to East Linton, about 20 miles from Edinburgh, where they bought the village stores. John Pettie showed an early interest in drawing and made surreptitious sketches of customers in his father's shop, or passers-by in the street; he sketched constantly. When he was sixteen Alison took him to Edinburgh to see James Drummond for advice about art training for the boy. Drummond, the son of an Edinburgh merchant, was then forty-two, a successful artist, and at the time of Alison's visit was librarian of the Royal Scottish Academy. At first, he tried to dissuade the young Pettie from becoming an artist, but changed his mind on seeing examples of his work. It was agreed therefore that John Pettie would begin study at the Trustees' Academy in October, 1855 and arrangements were made for him to lodge with Robert and Margaret Frier in Edinburgh for the duration of his studies.

Within two years the Friers were compelled by another expected addition to the family to move from Ratcliff Place to a larger house, and their second son, Robert Palmer Frier, was born in 1857 at 33 Dundas Street, the family's first house in Edinburgh's New Town. Until the end of the eighteenth century, the existence of the Nor' Loch and the adjoining marshy ground in the valley to the north of the Castle (now the site of Waverley Station), had prevented any expansion of the Old Town in that direction. But in 1767 the draining of the Nor' Loch and construction of a bridge over the marshland allowed the construction of a new town, designed on a gridiron plan by James Craig. Construction began in 1770 at the west end, with houses designed by the brothers Adam. After their deaths in the last decade of the eighteenth century the remainder of the houses were designed by others. In the 1820s a second new town was started, a little farther down the hill to the north. Like the first, it had three principal east-west streets, with others crossing at right angles – 'the draughty parallelograms' – as the author R L Stevenson called them. The houses in the second new town, generally of five storeys including basement, were rather plainer in their appearance and less well built than those in the first New Town. Nevertheless, to live even in the second New Town in the mid-nineteenth century was still indicative of a middle-class income and position. Frier had finally shaken off his humble origins. For the first time since their marriage the Friers could afford a living-in maid as well as domestic help. At the age of thirty-eight Robert Frier had arrived.

As far as his painting was concerned, Robert was still an amateur, in spite of acceptances of his work at the annual exhibition of the RSA. But the presence for nearly seven years in his house of John Pettie, with his considerable artistic ability even as a student, was to have a profound effect not only on Robert but on the whole family. Jessie Frier was eight when Pettie arrived, and Harry six. Robert was intending to become a professional artist. The sixteen-year-old John Pettie was their resident art teacher, for as he learned at the Academy, so did they, from him, at home; they were all willing pupils.

In 1856 Robert had added the manufacture of stockings to his cloth business, and his prosperity increased. The pictures he painted in his spare time sold readily, and by 1858 he was being paid as much as £10 or £12 each for them. Nevertheless the income from his painting was still insufficient on its own and the manufacture of stockings continued. Gradually, however, under the influence of Pettie's guidance, Robert began to gain a reputation as a landscape painter. Three or four of his pictures were accepted each year for exhibition at the Royal Scottish Academy, and they were often sold before the exhibition opened. The family moved again in 1859, to India Street on the west side of the second New Town, into a house built at the north end of the street on a massive 12 metres (40 feet) high plinth which maintained the level of both the street and the houses on land which sloped steeply down towards the woods which bordered the Water of Leith.

John Pettie moved with the family to their new home, and it was while there that the sketching club of which Pettie was later to be a distinguished member in London, came hesitantly into existence. Pettie would bring home some of his fellow pupils, and they would decide on a subject for the evening, such as 'Envy', 'Cowardice' or 'Honesty', and in the space of a couple of hours would try to give the idea substance in the form of a sketch or a painting. At about nine o'clock, Mrs Frier provided supper and then the group discussed their work, often far into the night. Robert Frier, although more than twice the age of the others, joined in enthusiastically, and it is likely that the young Harry was sometimes allowed to participate, at least until suppertime.

Harry was now ten years old. In common with other upper and middle-class children at this time, his primary education was conducted at home by his mother. From the earliest age he and Jessie had been given a grounding in drawing and painting by their father, a useful foundation for John Pettie's more advanced instruction. In 1857, Pettie's first submission to the annual exhibition of the Royal Scottish Academy was rejected, but in the following year, at the age of nineteen, he not only won a prize at the Trustees' Academy, but had his first picture accepted by the RSA. Two years later, he completed his studies at the Trustees' Academy but stayed with the Friers at India Street for another year while he studied anatomical drawing, and prepared illustrations for *Family Worship*, a devotional magazine published by Blackies in weekly parts.

Robert Frier finally relinquished control of the stocking factory sometime in 1860. It was in that year, having apparently sold his interest in the business, that he became a full-time professional creative artist, producing landscapes, portraits and topographical scenes in oils and watercolours. He rarely seems to have painted the genre pictures that were later considered so typical of the period. He also took pupils for drawing and painting. From this year on, Robert Frier 'went in for art as a profession' and encouraged every member of his family to follow him. None was excluded from instruction once old enough to hold a pencil, and the house in India Street came to resemble a communal painter's studio, for in addition to giving instruction to his family, Robert Frier was visited there by his other pupils as well. John Pettie stayed on with them after his anatomical course was finished, but with the arrival of another daughter, Margaret Elizabeth, always known as Maggie, it was no longer convenient for him to lodge there. In any case, the offices of *Good Words* for which Pettie was also providing illustrations were moved to London in 1862. Pettie had first visited London in 1858 where he had been much impressed by Turner's works in the National Gallery. In 1860

his first work had been hung at the Royal Academy, and his second in the following year, and so in 1862 he severed all connection with Edinburgh and moved to London.

In April of the year in which Pettie moved to London, Alice Margaret Frier, twin sister of Mary, then aged eight, fell ill, and within a few days had died of peritonitis. Her death was a shock to Harry, an impressionable twelve-year-old who was very fond of little Alice; it took a long time for him to recover from the loss.

It is likely that Harry was sent out to school when he was eleven years old. There were several private schools near his home, including one in India Street kept by a Mr Henderson. R L Stevenson, the author, who was a year older than Harry, attended it, and it may be that the two boys met, but if they did, neither has thought fit to place it on record. There was another school in Frederick Street, also in the New Town, and there was, of course, Queen Street Ladies' College, managed by the father of James Pryde, later to become well known as an artist of the Glasgow School, although it is unlikely that Harry was a scholar there! As far as his secondary education is concerned, however, all that is known is that he was not educated at any of Edinburgh's well-known public schools, but it is clear that he nevertheless received a good general education.

After leaving school, Harry sat for the entrance examination to the Edinburgh School of Art. There was never any doubt but that he would become a painter: it was the inevitable outcome of his father's ambition to profit from the demand for pictures, of the influence of John Pettie's teaching, and of a talent for the techniques of drawing and painting that he had acquired. The same had also been true of his older sister, Jessie, whose first picture had been exhibited at the RSA in 1863 when she was only seventeen. By 1866 she was already earning a reputation as a landscape painter. Only 20 students a year were accepted for training at the School of Art, but Harry passed the entrance examination, and in October 1867 was enrolled for a three-year course during which drawing and painting, perspective and composition were taught and practised.

As Robert Frier's artistic output increased, so did his prices and his reputation as a landscape painter, so that in 1868 he was able to improve his social position once more by moving into the first New Town, to 62, Queen Street, and by increasing the number of living-in servants to two. The houses in Queen Street were nearer to the city centre and had the additional benefit of unobstructed views across the countryside to the north; on a clear day the occupants could see across the Firth of Forth to the hills of Fife and Clackmannan. On the opposite side of the street were Queen Street Gardens, the use of which was reserved for the householders of Heriot Row to the north, where R L Stevenson lived as a boy at No. 17. An island in the lake in the gardens is said to have formed the basis for his *Treasure Island*. Sadly it was at 62 Queen Street that Harry's younger brother Robert died of chronic liver disease at the age of twelve in 1869.

Twenty years after his death, Sir David Wilkie (1785–1841) was still the guiding star of Scottish painting, in spite of the fact that it was his style of genre painting that was so much despised by the pre-Raphaelites when they dropped their mighty stone into the still pool of English art in 1848. It was not until the late 1860s, however, that the Scottish art establishment was gently rocked by the dying ripples of pre-Raphaelitism. The influence on Harry and his fellow students at the School of Art of pre-Raphaelite early work, such as the 'Church at Ewell' by Holman Hunt is quite noticeable. Harry's work showed a precision of manner, delicacy of detail and almost total lack of impasto which was characteristic of the pre-Raphaelites, and he, like them, had learned to create atmosphere by the imaginative handling of chiaroscuro and the employment of a full range of tones. But Harry never adopted the vividness and brilliance of the pre-Raphaelites' palette, nor the extraordinary flesh tones of some of their later work. Although his interiors and portraits glowed with fresh warm colours, they were never garish.

Successful practitioners in any field of endeavour are not, as a rule, directed into it. They are driven by an inner compulsion to devote all their energies to it for every waking hour of every day – witness the adolescent Pettie's constant surreptitious sketching under the shop counter, for example. This inner compulsion may be greatly discouraged by a realisation of one's inadequacy in the chosen field; what may have begun in a spirit of unquenchable enthusiasm becomes banal toil, or the endeavour may be abandoned altogether. Harry probably realised during his training at the Edinburgh School of Art that although, as an oil painter, he was technically competent, he lacked that spark of creativity which distinguishes the artist from a painter. Perhaps not. Maybe the standard of tuition was so inadequate that the creative aspect of an artist's training was neglected in favour of the purely practical. Creativity may be instilled on rare occasions by an especially inspirational teacher, who may succeed in sowing a seed which flourishes in a receptive pupil's

mind. Harry was not born creative and seems to have had no inspirational tutors. When he left the School of Art he was a competent painting technician, not an artist.

The completion of his course at the School of Art in the summer of 1870 coincided with the appearance of an advertisement for part-time art teachers at George Watson's College in Edinburgh. This institution had been founded in 1723 as Watson's Hospital by the first Accountant of the Bank of Scotland, but in September 1870 it was reformed and opened as a fee-paying school for 1000 boys. Both Robert and Harry answered the advertisement, and both were appointed, Robert at a salary of £80 (£3600 today) per annum, Harry at £60 (£2700). The duties were not onerous, being an hour or two each day, but their salaries were proportionately more than those paid to teachers in other disciplines, who received £150–£200 (the equivalent of £7000–£9300 today) a year for full-time work. In 1871 George Watson's Ladies' College was established in George Square, to the south of the Old Town, and Robert and Harry were appointed to part-time posts there also. By 1874 Robert was paid £100 (£4500) by GWC and £80 (£3600) by GWLC, while at the same time Harry received £60 (£2700) and £50 (£2250).

After he left the School of Art, at the age of twenty-one, Harry attended life-drawing classes at the Royal Scottish Academy for 102 evenings each year. At this time the famous George Chalmers and William MacTaggart were visiting tutors at the Academy School. They had been pupils of Robert Scott Lauder at the old Trustees' Academy, and from them the young Harry learned well. Among his contemporaries at the classes were J C Noble (1846–1913), who was elected Associate of the RSA in 1892, J R Reid (1851–1926), John White, Robert McGregor, E H Murray and A M Macdonald. This group of young men of whom Harry was one, presented both in Edinburgh and, later, in London, something of the aspect of a 'school'. Murray and Macdonald came to nothing and dropped from sight. McGregor followed an independent course, but Noble and the others were close companions and for some years their pictures were marked by very similar characteristics. The subjects they chose were of the simplest: country folk or children set in old gardens and orchards, at cottage doors, or in the village street, and their treatment was marked by an increase in the perception of values, fullness of tone, and vigour of handling, but with an inclination towards lumpiness of form. After a few years all four began to develop individual tendencies, Harry and Noble for example, making the figure element less prominent, and by stages becoming landscape painters.

While they were attending the RSA life-drawing classes, Noble and Harry Frier went to London to visit the National Gallery and Harry's cousin John Pettie at his studio. When he first went to London, Pettie had shared lodgings in Pimlico with W Q Orchardson (1835–1910) and Tom Graham (1840–1906), but on his marriage to Elizabeth Bossom in 1865, Pettie moved to Gloucester Road near Regent's Park. At this time Pettie's work was much in demand and he was gaining a reputation as a historical painter, although he was not elected a Royal Academician until 1874 to fill the vacancy caused by the death of Sir Edwin Landseer. Noble and Harry marvelled at Pettie's large studio, examined his work in progress, discussed with him his dislike of using gamboge, gave him the news from Edinburgh, and after a few days' stay returned to Scotland.

At the end of his first year at the Academy School in 1871, Harry won second prize for life drawing, but in the following year he took first prize. The first recorded sale of one of his oil paintings was in 1870 when the Royal Scottish Academy bought one of his entries in their annual exhibition for their own collection. It was later disposed of, and its present whereabouts is unknown. This purchase gives a slight indication of Harry's standing at the time; the RSA usually paid from £100 (£4500 today) to £200 (£9000) for a large painting by a well-known artist, and up to £30 (£1350) for an oil painting by a man of lesser standing, such as Robert Frier, but Harry's picture was sold for £2 (£90 today).

In April 1871 Harry described himself to the census enumerator as a 'figure painter', that is a portrait painter, and in 1873 he was renting a studio at 10 George Street in Edinburgh's New Town. The studio was probably no more than a small room on the third floor, but it faced north and provided a workplace within three minutes walk from home. He was now a man of twenty-four, just over six-feet tall, with reddish hair and the customary full beard of the time. His speech was quiet but firm and his Scots accent almost undetectable; it was not considered then to be indicative of the middle classes to speak with a distinct brogue. He was patient, slow to anger, and quick to right a wrong, but nevertheless still immature and irresponsible in outlook. He enjoyed spending long periods in idleness or in the company of his sisters Maggie and Mary, of whom he was especially fond. He counted time with his sisters as time well spent. When he was in the mood for work, he threw himself into it with enthusiasm, not letting anything stand in the way of its completion, but when it was finished, a spirit of indolence would overcome him once more.

It was at this time, when he was beginning to sell some of his work in the same way as his father had started nearly twenty years earlier, that Harry's career almost ended. He was descending the gangplank of a ferry behind a passenger who had shouldered his umbrella like a rifle. Harry stumbled and the ferrule of the umbrella entered his right eye so far as to cause physical damage to the eyeball and to cause complete loss of sight in that eye. That such a misfortune should befall an artist on the threshold of his career was a serious matter. He could no longer see in three dimensions and so was quite unable to tell, for example, how far the end of his brush was from the canvas, a matter of some importance when deft touches of colour were required to be applied with the brush held at arm's length. After the initial shock had subsided and the physical damage healed, Harry set about mastering his condition. Fortunately the disability was one that with practice could be overcome. A B Houghton, Sir John Tenniel and George du Maurier were other nineteenth-century artists who suffered in like manner. They all found difficulty in spatial measurements, of course, but noted an increased power of observation in the remaining eye. They also all suffered increasingly in the other eye as they grew older. So successful was he at overcoming his disability that Harry was for the first time able to support himself solely by creative painting and from commissions. He resigned his teaching post at George Watson's College in 1875 and, in February 1876, from the Ladies' College also. Although he was good-looking, there are no grounds for supposing that Harry was asked to resign, as was Samuel Austin (1796–1834), an art teacher at a Liverpool girls' school who was dismissed simply on the grounds that he was too handsome. As Harry said in his letter of resignation, he was leaving 'to engage in art'. He received a salary of £60 for his last year's teaching and moved to a larger studio in Hanover Street; later in 1876 he moved again to a studio at 37 George Street. At a time when portraiture was the only available means of recording a likeness in colour, there was little need for creativity in its production. Harry's prizes for portraiture are indicative of his competence in that field, and, given a steady flow of clients and moderate charges for a true likeness competently executed, portrait painting, supplemented by teaching, should have sufficed for him to make a living in any of the larger Scottish towns or cities.

Harry's father continued to teach part-time at both colleges, and in 1877 was assisted at the Ladies' College by Harry's sister Mary, then twenty-three years old, who like her brother and sisters had been taught drawing and painting at the Frier home academy. She was paid no salary for her work, because her duties were limited to taking classes when her father was unwell, a frequent occurrence at this time.

When he resigned from George Watson's College in 1875 Harry was beginning to make a name for himself. He had exhibited three oil paintings every year at the RSA since 1870. They were either genre subjects, street scenes or, more usually, portraits. In 1872, for example, he exhibited a portrait of his father, and in 1873, a portrait commissioned by an Edinburgh merchant, but from 1875 onwards he turned increasingly to the painting of landscapes, usually based on sketches made while he was on family holidays. In 1874, with the exception of Jessie who was visiting John Pettie in London, the family stayed at Finlarig, near Killin, and Robert, Harry and Jean, then aged twenty-two, all showed landscapes painted there in the 1875 RSA Exhibition. Other family holidays were spent at Tarbert on Loch Fyne, at Loch Goil and at Largo, Pittenweem and Leven in east Fife, during which pictures were produced for exhibition.

The present whereabouts of Harry's pictures of this period is unknown, except for one, a genre oil painting called 'A private examination'. Painted in 1875, it was bought for the unusually large sum of £45 (£2000 in modern values) from the RSA Exhibition by James Marson, and given by him two years later to the Art Gallery at Warrington. His father and his sister Maggie modelled for the picture, a typical genre painting of the period. The predominant colours are dark browns and fawns, but the highlights on the faces of the figures reflect the warm glow of the fire, and the brightness in the girl's bonnet completes the full range of tones. Harry signed the picture, as he almost always did, with his full name and date.

In the mid-1870s the country was plunged into an economic depression. At first Harry's life was unaffected. In May 1875 Harry's student friend John Noble was married, and in December after having a picture accepted by the the Glasgow Institute of Fine Arts, Harry's younger sister Jean married Hector Chalmers, then a lithographic draughtsman. The wedding was a splendid affair with a reception at the Alma Hotel in Princes Street. In 1876 and again in 1877 Harry's work was accepted, shown and sold at the RSA's annual exhibition, but the collapse in 1878 of the Glasgow City Bank had immediate and far-reaching economic consequences throughout industrial and commercial centres in Scotland. Unemployment became widespread and, for the first time for nearly thirty years, there was poverty and hardship. No longer was money available for picture buying. Suddenly there was barely enough to live on. Those 'amateurs who had gone in for art as a profession', borne up on the rising tide of economic prosperity, were left stranded as that tide ebbed.

All the family were affected. Harry's father continued teaching part-time at both colleges, but because the demand for studio pictures was so diminished, even he was beginning to find himself in financial difficulty. Harry's younger sister, Maggie, then a mere sixteen years old, was pressed into service and found a teaching post at George Watson's Ladies' College as her father's assistant. She was more than an assistant in fact, for she was responsible for almost all the art teaching there. It was for this reason that Robert, although nominally in charge of the art instruction at both colleges, received a salary of only £35 (£1750 today) from the Ladies' College, compared with £100 (£5000) from George Watson's College. In 1878, in order to be paid a salary, Mary taught French as well as acting as her father's standby, but she gave up both posts in the following year when she found full-time employment elsewhere. With Maggie's assistance, Robert continued to teach at both colleges until ill health compelled his resignation from the Boys' College in 1885 at the age of sixty-six. He was given a very generous honorarium of £100 (£5000). For a short time he continued as titular drawing master at the Ladies' College, although Maggie was actually supervising the classes, but this arrangement ended soon afterwards. In 1889, however, his health having improved, Robert was re-appointed to the Ladies' College, and continued to teach there until his death in September 1893, when Maggie was formally appointed in his stead.

Of all the family it was Harry who was most affected by the economic depression. He had resigned his teaching post at just the wrong time: his reputation as an artist was not yet sufficiently established, nor did his father command sufficient influence to secure commissions by which Harry might earn his living as a portrait painter. When money is short only the wealthy commission portraits, and in 1878 they were in a position to choose men of experience and reputation, G P Chalmers, Sir Daniel Macnee, James Irvine – but not Harry Frier. No, Harry was beginning the only career for which his upbringing and training had prepared him at the very time when economic circumstances were preventing him from earning a living by its means. Considering the future of his career, now for the second time put in jeopardy, Harry determined on a way out of his situation. He would move from the restricted provincial Scottish market to the broad plains of opportunity; he would follow Pettie, Noble, White and Reid and move to London.

# The Dyer Family

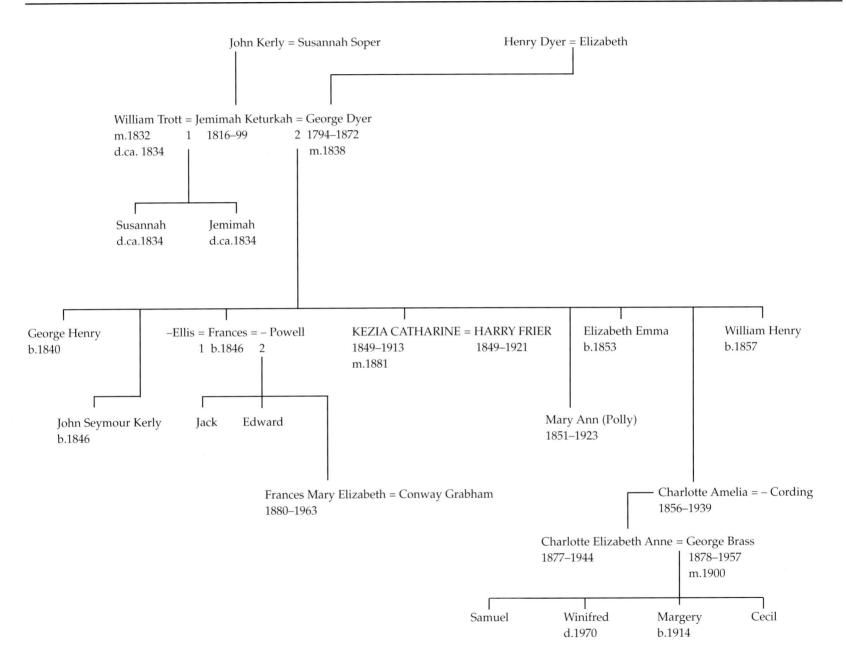

# London

Harry left Edinburgh for London in the late spring of 1878. By that summer he was established in lodgings at Oakley Street in Chelsea, from where he sent two genre pictures to Edinburgh for the RSA exhibition. In 1879 he moved a short distance to King's Road and submitted four pictures for exhibition in Edinburgh, two of which were sold before the exhibition opened. Apart from this, little is known of his life in London. What is clear, however, is that the breakthrough to success eluded him. He had emigrated to the south, perhaps not realising the extent of the recession or his lack of ability in comparison with more established portrait painters, for he had nothing original to offer. Lacking contacts and in the face of competition from more able and experienced practitioners, he failed. His regular submission of pictures for exhibition in Edinburgh, for several years after he had severed all connection with the city, suggests that he lacked initiative and that his work was moderately successful only in that environment. He should neither have given up the security of his teaching posts, nor have left Edinburgh.

None of his work was accepted for exhibition at the Royal Academy. Presumably he hawked his work round the private galleries and artists' agents in London, but with little or no success. He felt crushed and dispirited. Like Pettie before him, perhaps even through his influence, for Pettie was then approaching the summit of his career, Harry seems to have obtained some work as illustrator. A handful of carefully-drawn pen and ink drawings, sparing of line and with delicately worked shadows has been seen, but are now lost. They were reminiscent of magazine illustrations, book plates or birthday cards. Stylistically they date from this period and well illustrated his skill as a draughtsman. They were signed only with his monogram.

In order to produce work for sale more quickly and cheaply, he turned to the medium of watercolour. In 1880 he showed a single watercolour drawing, 'Shelling beans', at the Glasgow Institute of Fine Art, while to the RSA he sent three oil paintings. Some success, and regular employment came to him in 1879, if tradition is correct, when he obtained work as a scene painter at a London music hall. Apparently he adapted to the technique well, and was kept busy not only as a scene painter, but also as a stagehand. He was also often employed by the chorus girls to conceal holes in their tights by painting over them. One of the girls for whom he performed this service was Kezia Catharine Dyer, known as Kate. She was three months younger than Harry, having been born on 22 August 1849, the fourth child of George and Jemimah Dyer of Creech St Michael, near Taunton. Her father was at various times farmer, butcher and labourer, probably in that order, for he was a litigious man. Kate's mother, Jemimah, was the daughter of an estate worker at Whitestaunton Manor near Chard. She was first married in 1833 to a cordwainer at North Petherton. By him she had twin girls, but both the girls and their father were dead within four years. She married George Dyer at the church of St Mary Redcliffe in Bristol in December 1837, and the couple had eight children, five of whom were girls. George Dyer died in 1872 leaving Jemimah some small properties at Bathpool and a cottage called Thornybier, in which she lived, between the canal and the railway about a mile east of Creech St Michael. George Henry Dyer, one of Kate's brothers was in South Africa and another, John Seymour was a private in the Royal Marines. Her third brother, William Henry, was an agricultural labourer at Creech Heathfield. Most of her sisters were in service in London, although one later married and went to Australia where her husband sold her to a Chinaman by whom she was reputed to have had ten children. Charlotte, one of Kate's younger sisters, had an illegitimate daughter in 1877. A year or two later she married a sailor called Cording, but he seems to have died or disappeared shortly afterwards and thereafter Charlotte and her daughter Lottie lived with Jemimah at Creech St Michael.

Kate was apparently the only one of Jemimah's daughters to go on the stage. According to a rambling autobiographical account written

*Kezia Catharine Dyer in theatrical costume, c.1876.* A tinted carte-de-visite taken by a photographer in Islington, London.

*Jemimah Keturkah Dyer, Kate's mother, aged about sixty.* Photograph taken, c.1876.

by Jemimah Dyer in 1887, containing notes on each of her children, Kate was shrewd, avaricious and worldly but she was pretty and had a fine singing voice. It was probably late in 1879 when Harry and Kate fell in love. It is possible that Kate deliberately set out to catch Harry, in the belief that this thirty-year-old artist would provide her with the good things in life. He must have seemed quite a catch. He came of a good moneyed family, he was tall, handsome and a fastidious dresser, full of cheerfulness and good humour. As Kate saw it, Harry was on the threshold of a distinguished career like his cousin

John Pettie. Her own career prospects on the other hand were uncertain and her work irregular. Even when she was working she was poorly paid, so an alliance with Harry promised not only a considerable improvement in her circumstances, but a secure future. Their courtship lasted into the spring of 1880, when they became engaged. It was in that year that Harry came to Somerset for the first time when he and Kate visited Jemimah at Creech St Michael and Harry painted 'Interior in Somersetshire'. This was exhibited at the RSA that summer, when Harry and Kate went to Edinburgh to stay with

Harry's parents. The visit was a disaster. It seems that Harry's mother suggested to Harry that he would be foolish to throw himself away on such a low-class girl. Persuasion availed nothing, and in an atmosphere of ill will and recrimination, Harry and Kate left. As far as is known they never saw Harry's family again.

Harry and Kate returned to Somerset, united by their love. In the autumn they returned to London to work for the winter season in the music hall. In late February 1881 they returned to Taunton and stayed at the Old Angel Inn, from where they were married on 1 March at Taunton Registry Office. Thus was Harry trapped by Kate. Her scheme, if such it was, afforded her little comfort, however, for she spent much of the rest of her life an impoverished, childless and embittered woman, later despising and finally afraid of the man she had striven so earnestly to win.

*Kate Dyer, c.1879.* A carte-de-visite taken by a photographer in Knightsbridge, London.

In later life Harry claimed not only that he was of French descent but that he knew Paris well. Certainly the name Frier is of French derivation. Perhaps his forebears fled that country in 1685 after the revocation of the Edict of Nantes, whereby French protestants were deprived of civil and religious liberty, but whether the rest of his claim was designed to impress his audience, or whether the story of a sojourn in Paris had any basis in fact, cannot now be determined. His sisters Mary and Maggie had undoubtedly visited Normandy as they both submitted pictures of Pont Audemer to the 1879 RSA exhibition. Perhaps Harry and Kate went to France for their honeymoon, for neither was included in the census taken a month after their marriage. Perhaps they lived in that country for a

time, as no pictures of Somerset by Harry have been recorded for 1881 or 1882, and very few for 1883. He exhibited three pictures at the RSA in 1881, two genres and a landscape of Pittenweem in Fife. In 1882 he showed only one canvas there, 'Apple gathering in Somersetshire', for which he gave as his address 62 Queen Street, Edinburgh. Presumably he sent the picture to his sisters to submit on his behalf, for he had no studio in Edinburgh after 1877.

*Kate Frier.* A photograph taken at about the time of her marriage in 1881 and closely resembling a portrait of her painted by Harry Frier in the same year, now lost.

By the end of 1882 Harry must have realised that the most he would achieve by his painting could be decent mediocrity. He might not starve, neither would he earn significant recognition as his fellow students Noble, Reid and White were then doing. The question of his future began to press for an answer. His work was not good enough to allow him to remain with a new wife and perhaps a family, in the fiercely competitive environment of London or Paris. He was alienated from his family and home, so Edinburgh was closed to him: in any case the economic pressures that had caused him to quit the city nearly five years before still persisted, so there would be little prospect of earning a living there either. Jemimah Dyer suggested to Kate that she and Harry should come to live near her and care for her in old age. Harry realised that such a move might solve his difficulty. As an artist in a provincial town, with little or no professional competition, he should prosper, his wife would be content, and by this means they could perhaps both resume the style of living to which Harry had formerly been accustomed. They would move to Taunton.

# Taunton

Harry and Kate settled in Somerset some time in 1883. Kate's mother, Jemimah, removed from her house at Thornybier to a larger cottage she owned in Hyde Lane, not far from the crossroads at Bathpool. Possibly Harry and Kate lived with her there, or perhaps in the cottage adjoining which Jemimah also owned. At the same time Harry rented a room over Job Dyke's millinery shop at 5 East Reach, Taunton, for use as a studio, and to which he could invite potential customers to see his work.

At once the pressing need for a regular income made itself felt. Harry set about making contacts from whom he could solicit commissions. He began to frequent the better public houses, where he had no difficulty in making the acquaintance of the members of the town's trade and business community. Curiously, he does not seem to have advertised in any of the local papers of the day. There is a persistent rumour that Harry was a Freemason and there is no doubt that membership of the craft would have been an advantage to him at this time, but the rumour cannot be confirmed. Early in their relationship Harry had painted a head-and-shoulders oil portrait of Kate, about 45 x 135cm in size, a finely wrought work in sombre hues. It shows Kate, very self assured, wearing a dark brown dress trimmed with white lace, a gold locket of great beauty at her throat. Round her forehead a wide beige lace trimmed band contrasts well with her brown hair and fresh complexion. She is young, beautiful and there is just a suggestion of a smile at her lips. The portrait was displayed on an easel in the East Reach studio as proof of Harry's ability as a portrait painter, by which means he intended to earn a living.

At a time when social distinction counted for much, an educated man with a lower-class wife was unclassifiable. His slight Scots accent, unusual name and even more unusual occupation ensured that as far as Taunton was concerned, he remained an outsider, an oddity, and as a painter, a loner. Not only was a portrait painter someone unusual in the town – T G Crump had retired by this date, Henry Trood, the deaf and dumb painter, devoted himself with great success to painting dogs, and Francis Colthurst, who was later to earn a considerable reputation, had not yet begun his career – but in the continuing economic depression of the eighties, the moneyed classes had little inclination to commission portraits from an unknown Scots parvenu. Harry's isolation from the community was further emphasised by the indifference of the lower classes who, for the most part were inhibited from befriending him by his obviously middle class background.

He did receive one satisfying commission in 1884, to paint a group portrait in oils, 60 x 90cm. For this he selected as a background a view of the town seen from the south bank of the Tone near Priory, about 800 metres east of St James' Church. The Marks family of Lambrook Farm were portrayed as if resting from haymaking at lunchtime on a brilliant June day. On the left of the scene a waggon stands in the midst of a pile of tangled hay which catches and reflects the golden summer light. Behind the haycart is the hedge of Priory Path with four tall elms rising from it, while in the centre and on the right, the sweep of the River Tone coming to Obridge Lock glistens in the sunlight; birds fly low over the water to catch the innumerable insects in the shimmering heat. Reflected in the water are the towers of the town's churches, rather out of proportion, and hazy clouds high in the dazzling blue sky. The family group, father, mother, son and two daughters, is placed in the lower-right quarter of the picture in such a way as to make one wonder whether this is not so much a portrait as a landscape with figures. The mother is seated on the grass at the right, her bonnet shielding her face from the sun, while on her left sits her very small daughter in a rich crimson dress. Father sits on her right facing us. Behind him, stands a boy of about ten with a hayrake over his shoulder, while to his right the second daughter in full-length dress and white cloth bonnet rests elegantly on her rake. In the centre of the group the plates and jugs for their lunch are spread on the ground.

The scene is brilliant with sunlit colour. In its painting Harry employed one of his favourite devices, the contre-jour technique. A painting of the setting sun, throwing the foreground into deep shadow, the edges being highlit, is often rightly criticised as the facile technique of the second-rate artist. In this picture the view looks towards the noonday sun, and uses reflected light with subtlety, and highlights with restraint, to create a chiaroscuro effect of great beauty. The signature and date in Harry's normal cursive hand, in red, is in an area of deep shadow in the lower left corner. It is to be hoped that the Gould family appreciated their portrait, although it may have taken time for them to come to terms with their appearance as mere props in a landscape instead of the picture's principal subject.

A successful picture, yes: but in economic terms, an utter failure. Its execution, necessitating several sittings by all the members of the family, would have taken more than two months, so that an economic fee would have been so high as to deter others from commissioning work, while the fee that the Gould family might have been willing to pay would have been insufficient for Harry to live on. Harry realised that for the third time he was likely to be denied the opportunity of following the calling for which he had been trained; it was clearly impossible for him to make a living in Taunton from portrait painting, regardless of how many commissions he might receive. The time-consuming medium of oil painting must be abandoned.

Harry was thus compelled to turn for his bread and butter to working in watercolour. It was not too difficult to complete a quarter Imperial (27.5 x 37.5cm) watercolour drawing in a day or two, and as he could sell it for between 10 and 15 shillings (the equivalent of £25 and £37.50 today) depending on its complexity, half a dozen such pictures sold in a week would enable him to live quite well. But not portraits, of course. Even in watercolour, portraits would take much longer to complete, as the technique was very demanding. No, the drawings must be of topographical subjects.

Accordingly he made in the open air a number of small watercolour sketches of local views: a labourer's cottage in Hyde Lane, views on the canal, Tanpits Farm at Bathpool. They have the freshness and spontaneity of treatment of work painted in the open air, a vigour often lost when the finished drawing is made in the studio. Armed with these sketches, Harry called on the larger houses on the outskirts of Taunton to solicit commissions from the occupants to paint a view of their house. By this means he obtained orders from farmers, gentlemen and others for large watercolour drawings of their houses. Occasionally he persuaded the client to pay for the inclusion in the view of portraits of their children, and sometimes of their domestic pets also; the figures were usually placed in the foreground, and often rendered curiously out of scale.

In this way Harry began slowly to build a reputation as a water-colourist; occasionally he painted portraits in this medium for his own enjoyment. In 1881, for example, he had painted a small water-colour portrait of his sister-in-law Charlotte's illegitimate daughter, Lottie, who was then four years old. There is in the composition of this portrait a certain artlessness, typical of much of his work, as if his impetuous desire to capture the mood of the moment allowed no time for considerations of composition. Lottie was about to leave the room when she was called back just as her hand was reaching for the door knob. She has just turned away from the door, her right hand still on the knob, her left arm cradling her rag doll. She looks a little puzzled, wondering what it is that Uncle Harry has called her for. Her calf-length crimson dress and flaxen hair are framed by the dark brown panelled door, which together with the boarded floor on which she stands, occupies much of the picture space. Hanging on the door is an old coat, beside it can be seen the corner of a child's chair, while on the left of the door, against the wall, a tablecloth is thrown carelessly over a basket. The viewpoint of the picture is at the level of Lottie's eye, and doubtless it was a present for her.

Whatever may have been his artistic shortcomings, there is no doubt that Harry was a prolific painter. Some indication of his entire output may be gained from a catalogue of nearly 600 of his works which has been made, and from an assessment of the average length of time needed to complete a single picture. Making allowance for those which have been destroyed or taken elsewhere – and many are known to have been taken to several Commonwealth countries, for example – a crude extrapolation suggests that his total output during the thirty-eight years he worked in Taunton, perhaps amounted to 2–3000 watercolours. As most of his pictures are dated, an approximate annual output may similarly be guessed at. On this basis it seems that he only painted 25–30 watercolours in 1884, 80–90 in 1885, but only 50–60 in 1887. There seems little doubt that Harry was only at peace when he was painting, and it was probably this that compelled him to carry on, indeed it was the only way in which he believed he could support himself. In spite of this his irresponsible attitude to life led to a relaxed approach to his work; he seems to have produced work sufficient in quality and quantity only to keep the wolf from the door.

In 1887 Harry paid for an entry in the Taunton Directory in which he is listed under 'Bathpool village, commercial section' as 'Artist and Landscape Painter'. It was in that year that he was commissioned to paint a view of the front of Clarke's Hotel, now the Castle Hotel, the first Taunton town scene he is known to have executed. Seen from Castle Green, the picture shows the front of the building covered with vivid green ivy, the colour of which has been changed as a result of the action of light. In the foreground are several horse buses and a scatter of figures, but most of this area is occupied by the shadow of a building just out of view to the right, thus effectively drawing the eye to the principal subject. This view is characteristic of his work of this period in having a foreground empty save for a few figures added almost as an afterthought. This was as a result of the influence of scene painting, for in the painting of theatrical backcloths space must be left in the centre and lower portion of the scene, so that the actors are clearly visible against a background uncluttered by detail. Without the horse buses and figures this view of Clarke's Hotel could well have served as such a backcloth. Indeed it is possible that in this instance the foreground interest was added at the client's request, as had happened in the watercolour view of Creech St Michael street painted in 1885. In that case there were no figures in the scene at all, but later a horse and cart led by a labourer was added in gouache; traces of the original work may still be seen through the added figures.

Harry's mother Margaret, died in 1888 of 'heart disease and general dermatitis' at her home at 108 George Street, Edinburgh to which she and Robert had moved in the previous year. A large house in the principal street of Edinburgh's first New Town, immediately to the north of Princes Street, 108 had a slight claim to fame in that it was the house in which Sir Walter Scott had lived for four years after his marriage in 1797 to Charlotte Carpenter, the daughter of a refugee from the French Revolution. Ninety years later, however, the ground floor was occupied by business premises and the upper floors were divided into flats, presumably all that Robert and Margaret could afford in their reduced circumstances. In view of Margaret's profound disapproval of Kate Frier, it is unlikely that either Harry or Kate would have attended her funeral. In like manner the marriage in June 1889 of John Pettie's daughter Alison to Hamish McCunn, a minor Scots composer and conductor, now remembered almost solely for his overture 'Land of the Mountain and the Flood', passed Harry by. He was by this date quite isolated from his former home, his relations and old friends, too busy trying to support himself to be much aware of or interested in what was happening in London or Edinburgh.

On 8 March 1889 the centre of Taunton was flooded, (as it has been on numerous occasions before and since), to a depth of several feet in the low-lying areas of Bridge Street and Station Road. During this period of flooding, on a Friday night, Pollard's timber yard and buildings in Wood Street caught fire and were much damaged. T Goldsworthy Crump, the artist's son, was there and photographed the scene. The *Illustrated London News* made an engraving from Crump's photograph, and during the next thirty years, Harry Frier made several watercolour versions of the scene from either the photograph or the engraving. In some versions, there is a row of posts on the right of the street, on one of which an intrepid spectator stands, gazing at the bright glow in the centre of the fire. Others include a man in a skiff rowing up the street.

In the summer of that year Thomas Redler of Bathpool Mills commissioned Harry to paint a pair of watercolour views of his house and the mill. Throughout his working life Harry displayed a noticeable reluctance to portray anything of an industrial nature. Machinery, locomotives and automobiles never appear in his pictures; although he lived close to the railway for more than thirty years, it never once featured in his work. True he once painted a view of one of the swing bridges over the canal near Bathpool, but that was a pastoral rather than an industrial scene. In fact, the canal, along which he walked daily from Bathpool to his East Reach studio, was the subject of many of his watercolour drawings. The paintings for Redler of Bathpool Mill avoided giving indication of the building's purpose: Thomas Redler's house which adjoined the mill, was seen from the east, with a minimum of mill building, mostly concealed by foliage. In painting the view of the mill from the west, the viewpoint chosen was so far away that the few cows grazing in the field in the foreground might be mistaken for the picture's principal subject .

Commissions in 1890 included a large watercolour drawing of St George's Church at the upper end of Billet Street, a house on the north side of Bathpool crossroads, and another, location unknown, of which the gamboge constituent of the green has faded. The use of cheap pigments considerably accelerates the fading process which results from the exposure of watercolour drawings to light and Harry's use of them in a commissioned painting suggests that he was already short of money. It is not surprising that this was the year of his last known submission of an entry to the annual summer exhibition of the Royal Scottish Academy. In 1891 financial pressure compelled him to give up his studio in East Reach, and he and Kate, still childless, moved into Taunton to live at 11 Greenbrook Terrace, off Wood Street, in the artisan district close to Taunton's town centre.

After Harry's sister-in-law, Charlotte Cording, had lost her sailor husband soon after their marriage, she reverted to using her maiden name of Dyer. She earned a living by acting as an unofficial midwife, and it was possibly at about this period, in the early 1890s, that Charlotte's illegitimate daughter Lottie, came to live with the Friers for a time. A considerable bond of friendship was formed between Harry and Lottie, for when she was eighteen in 1895, he again painted her portrait. This time it was a head and shoulders in oils, 45 x 30cm in size, and it displays his mastery of both the medium and the genre. A finely wrought work, it shows Lottie in three-quarters view from her right, against an attractive blue-green background. The fresh complexion of her face is painted without impasto, and her auburn hair hanging in long ringlets is painstakingly detailed.

The move to Taunton and the relinquishing of his East Reach studio heralded an improvement in Harry's fortune. He found an outlet for his work in Alfred Vickery's artists' materials shop at 16 Bridge Street, near Laverock Court, on the site of the old theatre. His work was displayed for sale in the shop window and Vickery acted as Harry's agent in taking orders. Alfred Vickery was a colourful character who loved all things Scottish. He had taught himself to play the bagpipes, and later, when he knew Harry well, Alfred would parade up and down outside Harry's house, dressed in kilt and sporran, piping a lament.

As a result of the upsurge in tourism in the 1880s, Taunton became a centre for visitors who made excursions by horse bus to surrounding villages and the Quantocks. Harry's watercolour drawings were bought as souvenirs of their visits and sold quite well. He was asked for other topographical views also, and so from about 1892 he began to accumulate a stock of sketches about 17.5 x 27.5cm in size on cartridge paper, annotated with colours and points of detail, numbered, and often priced, and kept on shelves in a cupboard in the bedroom that served as his studio. By 1910 there were more than 900 sketches in the cupboard. A watercolour drawing could be made from any sketch by the traditional method of pricking through the salient points of the sketch on to another sheet of paper underneath, so that a new pencil drawing could quickly be made ready for rendering in watercolour. Sometimes enlargements were made by squaring up, and the original sketches are occasionally ruled off into squares for this purpose. Some of his sketches were reproduced by

him so much that he made tracing paper copies of them and continued to reproduce them by this means.

Some sketches seem never to have been reproduced in colour at all. A fine pair of sketches of a carrier's yard, entitled 'Round the corner, Purchase's, Wood Street', lively and vigorous drawings of a ramshackle house and yard, have only been seen in sketch form. They show a sensitively drawn two-wheeled farm wagon against a background of decaying brick and timber buildings. From the door of a gap-toothed boarded stable on the left, a horse looks out. Harness, wheels, broken shafts, a turnip cutter and water butts lie about the yard, and in the centre of one of the views stands a very small girl in a sun bonnet holding a basket. In drawings such as this, Harry shows a mastery of form and perspective, economy of line and deftly worked shadows. For a man with only one good eye he was an accomplished draughtsman, although he was not always satisfied with his own work. On a sketch of a house made in 1896, Harry has written in the sky: 'a mouldy sketch'.

Some of his larger landscapes were painted as speculative ventures, and often employed the contre-jour technique. An example of such a picture shows the view from what is now French Weir Park, looking south to St John's Church, which is near the left edge of the picture. A somewhat uninteresting prospect is improved by an exciting windy sky, a scatter of sheep, a well-rendered cow and a girl wearing a straw hat seated on the grass in the foreground. Signed and dated 1890 in red, it is marred only by Harry's failure to capture the feeling of movement of the falling water of French Weir on the extreme right. The satisfactory representation of movement, whether of water, as in this case, or of people and animals, was something that Harry never seems to have been able to master. For a professional painter this is surprising, but perhaps more so is the fact that he did not shrink from making the attempt. Watercolour is a demanding medium and, to succeed, the work should be fluid and transparent. In the main, Harry's pictures are neither, and it is for this reason that people seeing his work for the first time think that he must have been an amateur painter. Many watercolour drawings to his standard are shown and sell well today at local amateur exhibitions. In other respects too, his work betrays a curiously amateurish, almost childish quality: the symmetrical composition decorated with stock figures often repeated in entirely different pictures, the placing of foliage masses in the lower foreground corners, intended to direct the eye to the picture's principal subject, the lack of design in some drawings, which in some instances leads one to wonder what was the subject of the picture. All of these shortcomings, together with a constant naïvety of execution, point to his surprising immaturity as an artist.

These strictures should not be taken as being applicable to all his work. Many of his watercolour drawings were so successful in every respect, that one is astonished that they were painted by the same man. A watercolour of 1894 testifies to his success. It is a fresh sparkling view of Priory Lock, near Lambrook, constructed to allow river vessels to pass Obridge Weir. Although the drawing is only 25 x 17.5cm in size, it has that quality of sunlit radiance that is characteristic of his finest work, and which so quickly fades if his pictures are exposed too much to daylight. The tower of Trinity Church, daringly framed by tall elms flanking Priory Path, breaks the line of the sunlit Blackdown Hills. The firm geometric lines of the footbridge over the lock and of the penstock behind provide a satisfying contrast to the fluidity of the rest. The distant view is softly reflected in the gently moving water of the River Tone in the foreground, and the brickwork of the disused lock pound glows warm in the bright side-lighting. The peace and stillness can almost be felt.

Fourteen Taunton views have been recorded as being painted in 1891. As these probably represent about a quarter of his output for the year, it is an indication that he was busy. John Pettie, the wealthy and at the time famous historical painter, Royal Academician and Harry's cousin, died in 1893, at the early age of fifty-four. He was buried in Paddington Cemetery in London. Harry Frier, unknown, struggled on.

In 1892 Harry was commissioned to paint a view of the front of old Haydon Farm next to the Manor House in Bishop's Hull. A late medieval house with gabled dormers and a central front porch, the farm is depicted with a path leading straight to it from the front gate. On either side of the path were symmetrical lawns and flower beds with sunflowers in full bloom against the west boundary garden wall. In front of the porch, Harry painted the daughter of the house cradling her baby brother in her arms, but the client did not like it and insisted the figures be removed. The excision had to be made in body-colour and detracts from the finished picture.

During the summer of 1893, Harry completed a small watercolour drawing with the intention of submitting it for exhibition but he seems to have decided against doing so. A genre picture entitled 'Taking Stock', it shows a pensive farmer leaning on a gate watching some fowls scratching about in the yard in the foreground. It is

tempting to suppose that this rather gloomy picture may have been not only a deliberate attempt to portray the double meaning of the title, but perhaps also Harry saw something of himself in the farmer wistfully contemplating his own lack of that success which had come so early and with such prodigality in the career of his late cousin John Pettie. Whatever may have been the deeper significance of this picture, as a genre painting it is almost entirely devoid of merit.

On 2 September 1893, Harry's father, Robert Frier, died while on a visit to Harry's friend from student days, J C Noble, at his home at Coldingham in Berwickshire. An announcement of his death, with portrait, was printed in the *Edinburgh Evening Dispatch* on 5 September and an obituary appeared in *The Scotsman* on 6 September. It said of him:

*…he was one whose influence in Scottish artistic circles… was neither small nor unimportant. Many will remember him as one of the oldest and most respected teachers of drawing in Edinburgh… Years ago, Mr Frier's house in India Street was a rallying point for artists young and old, and many a prominent artist of today owes not a little to the systematic instruction or kindly counsel from one whose special pride it was to be a teacher and guide to others. But it was always to John Pettie, his sister's son, that his mind returned as especially his own man, and it was an unfailing source of pride to him that it was through his efforts… that the future Royal Academician's introduction to art was effected…*

It is hardly surprising that this obituary notice, in its laudatory account of Robert Frier's artistic tutelage of John Pettie, should be at variance with the account given in Hardie's biography of Pettie which formed the basis for part of the first chapter of this account. Robert Frier was buried in the Dean Cemetery off Edinburgh's Queensferry Road where lie many other famous Scotsmen including the artists G P Chalmers and Sam Bough, both of whom had been Robert's friends.

Most of Harry's output during 1893 consisted of Taunton scenes, including a large commissioned view of Moor Farm, but during that summer he was painting in the open air on the Quantocks, on land owned by the Threxton family of Aisholt. Some ponies grazing nearby were, as so often happens, overcome with curiosity and crowded round his work, compelling Harry to abandon it and retreat. When he was able to return to collect the remains of his work, Harry wrote to the Thrextons complaining about the action of their beasts, and, doubtless with tongue in cheek, enclosed a bill for the damage. They paid in full, and Harry, with characteristic generosity, returned by way of receipt, a sketch of the incident in ink and pencil. The picture is not at all in Harry's usual style; the animals are quite well drawn, but very heavily shaded in ink, as are all the foreground details. A sense of distance is achieved by the use of lighter pencil shading in the background. It is signed, in ink, in the lower left corner with his monogram and date, and below, on the mount, Harry has written the title, 'Biting Criticism'.

It was at about this time that Harry became friendly with William Crockett the photographer, who lived at 26 Bath Place, and whose glass-roofed studio was in the garden behind. Crockett was born in Liverpool in 1851 and the two men may have become acquainted through Kate's sister Charlotte, who had worked for the Crocketts as a domestic servant in the eighties. They became firm friends and it may well have been at Crockett's suggestion that Harry began to produce monochrome watercolours in imitation of photographic prints. The employment by Harry of the technique of using Chinese stick ink as a medium began in 1892 and increased in 1893 to two-thirds of his recorded output and to more than four-fifths in 1894 when, of 16 recorded watercolour drawings, 14 were in monochrome. The stick of ink was dissolved in water and the resulting dark brown liquid filtered from one dish to another by capillary attraction through a woven cotton wick several inches long, to remove the sediment. The liquid was diluted with more or less water to produce a full range of tones in a brownish black colour. The technique was long established, but Harry had not tried it before, and by its means he obtained delicate effects of light and shade. As the work involved in producing a monochrome was almost as much as in any other watercolour drawing, there was little advantage in terms of cost to the buyer, and it is no surprise that in 1895 the proportion of monochromes in recorded drawings fell to a tenth, a level maintained for the next two years. Thereafter monochromes are rarely found, although Harry occasionally produced 'penny plain, twopence coloured' versions of the same scene.

Like Harry, Kate also suffered physical damage to one of her eyes. It happened in 1894, when she was being offered a flower to smell and it was accidentally jabbed into her left eye. The eyeball was damaged and the eyelid remained thereafter permanently semi-closed. Another account of the incident suggests an accidental blow by Harry, and yet another would have it that the accident resulted from a violent quarrel between them. Although this is unlikely, there is no

doubt that their relationship was not happy. In a 'letter to my dearest daughter Kezia Catharine Frier', included in Jemimah Dyer's long autobiographical dissertation written in 1887 and added to from time to time until her death, Jemimah wrote:

*My dear child, I now address a few lines to you and hope that you will think of me after I am gone from you. I often grieve, although I never tell you, to see you trying so hard to work for this world's goods and neglecting to work for another world, a better world… Don't say no bad words: disdain such actions. I am often broken down in heart when I see you so downhearted, and it hurts me, so many are the tears I have shed when you are not where I am. But we all got our troubles in this world. But my dear child, it grieves me so to think after all you do, you don't get a kind word…* from Harry presumably.

Regrettably four pages of the 'letter' are missing at this point, but when the manuscript resumes, the letter is still not quite finished. In a later addition to the manuscript, written in the spring of 1894, Jemimah refers to Kate's eye:

*But I trouble a great deal about her now as she is likely to lose her eyesight, and is always at present under medical treatment, and is now very thin and delicate. I am awfully grieved about this oftentimes, but I do hope and trust that she will regain her eyesight again, please the Lord.*

She did, but her eyelid was scarred for the rest of her life. Jemimah often visited her daughter and son-in-law. She occasionally stayed at their house, although, 'she is very kind to me, but my heart can't always be with them to stay long.' Clearly she did not get on with Harry. It is noticeable that in all the pages of her 'autobiography', Jemimah never once referred to Harry by name. The principal cause of friction between Harry and Kate arose from unfulfilled expectations. Harry married a pretty, vivacious girl who was going to bear him the children he so much wanted. Kate married a tall handsome artist, quite a catch for a country girl; a man who could paint portraits as well as that was bound to succeed. He would provide her with plenty of 'this world's goods'. Thirteen years later, both were disillusioned. There were never to be the children Harry wanted so much; the success and wealth for which Kate yearned never materialised. As Kate saw it, Harry shut himself upstairs all day painting pictures that did not sell. When he was not painting he was out enjoying himself, leaving her alone, short of money, with only a cat for company. Gradually she ceased to care, about the house, or the marriage, and finally, perhaps, about Harry. He became first cynical, then morose, treating Kate as little more than a servant, and as a form of escapism, he began to drink.

*Kate Frier, c.1895.* A carte-de-visite taken by Arnold, London Studio, Taunton.

*Harry Frier, c.1895.* A carte-de-visite taken by Arnold, London Studio, Taunton.

In 1895, possibly at Crockett's suggestion, the Friers moved from Greenbrook Terrace to Bath Place. Charlotte Dyer had in the previous year become housekeeper to F J Spiller, the jeweller, and it was one of his houses that Harry rented. Perhaps because the rent was higher than in Greenbrook Terrace, and because Harry was not really paying his way, they found themselves in difficulties, and in 1897 they gave up the house and moved back to Greenbrook Terrace, this time to No. 15, which was to be their last home.

Harry always worked upstairs in the front bedroom of No. 15. He did not insist on north light, but he refused to paint by artificial light, as it would distort colour values. His method of painting at this time was to mount dampened paper on an inclined drawing board, and, commencing with the sky, run fairly wet washes of blue and grey as needed, leaving areas of white paper for clouds. On one occasion he

was at work on a large landscape, and the sky was all swimming wet when Harry paused to take a pinch of snuff. Unfortunately, the snuff was dropped into the middle of the wet sky, there followed an oath, and then: 'Ah, well! It will have to be a winter scene now,' and he dipped his brush into some neutral tint, mixed it with the snuff and turned what had been intended as a summer sky into an angry winter one. Only when the sky was complete and dry would Harry begin on the landscape, starting in the traditional manner with the hazy distant tints, working towards the foreground, completing each plane of distance before starting on the next. Figures and foreground details were added either as a separate operation on an area of paper left for them, or occasionally, but with increasing frequency as the years passed, added in body-colour or gouache on top of the completed foreground.

Harry's use of highly fugitive gamboge mixed with Prussian blue to make greens has caused many of his watercolours to fade to an overall dull blue. It is for this reason, and because he used the cheapest paper and mounts available, that many of his pictures are now in such poor condition. In addition, time and damp have caused deterioration of his watercolour drawings, which are often foxed and mildewed. When his drawings have been kept in folders away from the light, the fresh brightness of his palette comes as something of a pleasant surprise. This brightness of palette may still be seen in his oils, which are not affected by light to the same extent.

The ten years from 1895 to 1905 mark the period of Harry's best watercolour work. In 1895 he was thirty-six. Nevertheless he was still relatively immature and carefree in his approach to life. If he wanted, he worked: otherwise he went up to Scarlett's to gossip with his acquaintances. Harry and Kate could not afford to go away for holidays, but they often went to stay at Mary Ann Dyer's boarding house at Minehead. Kate's sister Mary Ann, always known as Polly, was reputed to have been the mistress of a London solicitor. It is said that he financed her boarding house in Minehead by way of recompense, and that he was a frequent visitor. It is also alleged that when Harry and Kate stayed there, often their only means of payment was in kind, with watercolour drawings, which Polly displayed for sale to other visitors.

In 1896 Harry painted a fine large pair of watercolours for the rector of Thornfalcon. They both showed the then old town bridge: one looked north from the brewery and had on the river in the foreground a string of three square coal barges as well as the rowing boat that he always included in his river scenes. The second was a view of the bridge from Coal Orchard, looking upstream. Both drawings are signed and dated, one in the lower left corner, the other in the lower right. It is said they were painted in lieu of repayment of a loan, but this seems unlikely. It was in this year too that Harry made a monochrome copy of a picture by another artist, at the request of a friend of the owner. The view was of Fingle Bridge over the River Teign near Chagford, and the original was painted by Jolier. The copy bears Harry's signature in the lower right corner, but on the back of the mount Harry wrote that it was a copy. This commission led in due course to a happy and profitable association with Charles Tite which was to last until Harry's death.

Charles Tite was born in Taunton in 1842 and became editor and later one of the proprietors of the *Western Flying Post* in Yeovil. In 1886 Tite sold his interest in the paper, and retired, first to Wellington, and then in 1896 to Taunton, where he lived first in Bishop's Hull Road and later in South Road. He became very interested in local history and archaeology, joining the Somerset Archaeological and Natural History Society in 1879. He became Secretary in 1900 and Vice President in 1913. He formed a collection of 6000 books either written by natives of Somerset or dealing with aspects of Somerset's history and topography. Part of this collection comprised Somerset prints, illustrations and portraits, most of which are now bound into folio volumes. Tite presented the entire collection to SANHS and it was kept in the Society's rooms at Taunton Castle, but is now held in the Society's room adjoining Somerset Studies Library. Tite found in Harry a willing paid assistant in his scheme for the recording of Somerset scenes and commissioned him over the

*Charles Tite.*

next ten or fifteen years to paint a series of watercolour drawings to add to the collection. Broadly speaking, these are either 'views' or 'characters'. In preparing the views, Harry was commissioned to make copies of old prints and pictures of Taunton, by Turle, for example, of Bridgwater by John Chubb, of Farringdon Gurney and other places. Perhaps outstanding among these is a sensitively wrought interior of one of St James' Almshouses painted just before their demolition in 1896. Successful and well executed though these are, they are perhaps not as interesting as the series of Taunton characters. These were prepared during the next twenty years, in colour, and were bound by Tite into albums thus preserving their freshness. In 1898, for example, Harry painted from a photograph Billy Brewer, the famous Taunton fortune teller who had died in 1890, the town crier, a constable of 1860 and Jimmy Morse, a one-armed rural postman. Thirty of these small portraits were painted, the last untitled, but dated 1919, which showed a man selling hot pies to a small boy.

In addition to the character sketches, Harry was asked to prepare sets of coloured and monochrome drawings such as 'Courts and Corners of Taunton' produced in 1903. They included plans and elevations of Huish's original almshouses in Hammet Street which had been demolished in 1868, and even architectural details such as the carved coat of arms over the east door of Gray's almshouses. In all Harry prepared 2–3000 watercolour drawings for Charles Tite, who generously allowed Harry to make copies to sell elsewhere as he could. Later when Harry was unable to support himself Tite allowed him a pension of 7s (the equivalent of about £18 today) a week.

At about the turn of the century, Harry made many small pen-and-ink sketches, lightly washed in the shadows with neutral tint, with highlights occasionally being picked out in white: views of St James Street almshouses , demolished in 1896, the old town bridge, which was to be rebuilt in 1896, and sketches of the narrow residential courts opening off St James' Street, High Street and East Street, a noted feature of the town at that time, so reminiscent of the wynds of Edinburgh's Old Town. The sketches are variable in quality, and in no way approach the vigour and precision of his pencil sketches. As they were often only 10 x 7.5cm in size, they could be dashed off in a couple of hours, and might sell for 2s (about £5 at today's prices). Many were bought by Charles Tite for his collection.

On 25 July 1897, Harry's youngest sister Maggie Eliza, who then earned her living by painting china, was married to her second cousin William Frier, a salesman based in Leeds. The couple settled in the northern suburbs of that city, and were later joined by Mary, Harry's other younger sister who remained unmarried. William and Maggie may have had a daughter, Kathleen Mary, and they lived in Leeds for the rest of their lives.

Twelve watercolours have been recorded as having been painted by Harry during 1897, suggesting a likely total output of between 50 and 60. Among them is a lovely little sketch of a 'Duckhouse on a Backwater', and a view of Taunton town mill seen from the north bank of the Tone, a copy of an earlier version of the same view. The mill building is prominent on the right, behind the brewery, with a small brick arched bridge in the centre of the picture. The privies of the houses which fronted on to North Street are on the left of the view, precariously perched on piles driven into the river bed. The warm colours of the brickwork and tiled roofs contrast well with the cool tints of the river in the foreground. The scene is side-lit from the west and the play of light and shade on the buildings contributes much to its interest. In spite of its technical merit the composition of this picture is unsatisfactory: the tiny arch carrying the road over the tailrace of the mill at the focus of the scene is not sufficiently dominant to unify the composition. Such an empty centre and the lack of cohesive design is common to many of his topographical drawings. The view of Clarke's Hotel, and of St John's Church and French Weir, for example, have also no central point of interest. The scene in both comprises many disparate elements, only the hotel building in the first and the sky in the other serving to pull the scenes together, but in both the result is equally unconvincing. Clearly, Harry rarely made the attempt to elevate competently rendered topographical views into works of art. Thus the interest of much of his work, superficially attractive though it is, lies in its appeal to students of local history and topography.

Just as he was at last beginning to break free from the influence of theatrical design, Harry was commissioned to paint the scenery for the production of the opera 'In the Days of Siege' written by Harold Jeboult, a native of Taunton and organist of St Mary's Church. The subject of the opera was a romantic love story set in Taunton just before the town was surrendered to Robert Blake during the Civil War. It was presented on three successive nights in the Assembly Rooms of the London Hotel (now converted into part of Marks & Spencer's store) in April 1898. Harry designed the largest proscenium and back-cloth ever erected in Taunton. The first scene was of the exterior of the old White Hart Inn, with the gabled houses on the west side of Fore Street and the opening into Bath Place behind. The second was of the courtyard of Taunton Castle by moonlight. At the top of the proscenium Harry painted Taunton's borough crest with scrolls; on one side of the arch was a panel containing a view from Priory showing the penstocks and Trinity Church in the distance, and on the other side a panel contained a view of St John's Church from the towpath above North Town bridge. 'Mr Harry Frier may be congratulated on the taste shown' wrote the critic in the *County Gazette*. Two years later the opera was revived and performances staged in aid of the Taunton Borough Fund for South African War Reservists. The same scenes as in the first production were used again, but in addition Harry painted a new drop scene which showed Taunton from Cotlake Hill which was 'extremely effective and much admired'.

Kate's mother came to stay for a week with the Friers at Greenbrook Terrace in July 1898, while Harry busied himself making an oil painting of Fingle Bridge, near Chagford, for William Crockett. Two genre pictures were painted during the year, perhaps for submission to an exhibition. One, entitled 'Evening at North Curry', is 35 x 25cm in size and contains some of Harry's favourite picture elements: a stream meandering from foreground to middle distance, two figures, and groups of trees in the middle distance silhouetted against the twilit sky, in which birds are flying. With the exception of the sky, the tones are so subdued that details are difficult to discern. It is, of course, possible that this effect could have been caused by the accidental deposition of snuff referred to earlier. The sky was painted in French ultramarine, a colour noted for causing clumping of pigment, resulting in a mottled effect which, sparingly used, is pleasing. In general the picture is so much overworked that all freshness and spontaneity has been lost. The contrast between the highly finished and over-elaborate drawings prepared for exhibition and the run-of-the-mill examples produced for local sale could not be more marked; nevertheless, most of his exhibition pictures are only known today because they remained unsold.

Harry painted another genre picture at this time, entitled 'Her pets'. This is the very antithesis of 'Evening at North Curry', for the scene is set in a summer garden in front of a barn, of which only a small part of the sunlit wall and the thatched roof are visible. A homely, naïve picture, it employs chiaroscuro to focus attention on the main subject.

For Charles Tite, Harry painted 'Path at Holway Farm, 1763' (some later versions painted for sale say '1764') in 1898. Several versions exist showing a girl dressed in brightly coloured eighteenth-century costume. In some she carries buckets hanging from a yoke; in others not. The significance of the title and date is not apparent, but it is a pleasing drawing.

After a long illness Kate's mother, Jemimah Dyer, died on 2 January 1899 and she was buried at Creech St Michael a few days later. She was eighty-four and like many Victorian country women had lived a long hard life. Her small properties were sold, and the proceeds divided into eight parts for her children. It is unlikely that in terms of 'this world's goods' Kate benefited much from her mother's demise.

The year of 1899 was productive for Harry as he probably painted and sold nearly 200 watercolours, most of which were of a high technical standard. It was in this year that he first painted two panoramic views of the town, each being 50 x 75cm size. The less successful of the two was a view from the rising ground near Lambrook to the east, and is of interest principally because the whole of the foreground and the middle distance has since been built over. Much more satisfying is the panoramic view from Cotlake Hill to the south of the town. This view encompasses the whole town from St John's Church on the west to King's College on the east, and is framed by trees. In the foreground girls are raking up hay for the men to load onto the waggon a little way off; coats and cider jugs have been left in the purple shade of the field hedgerow. This was the view which was employed for the scenery in the revival of Jeboult's opera in the following year. Other versions of the Cotlake Hill picture exist showing the same view at harvest time, with stooks of wheat in rows down the field, and there is an uncompleted version, probably painted in 1916, in which only the sky and part of the distant hills are in colour, but the remainder is precisely drawn with careful pencilled shading in the shadowed areas.

A stay with Polly Dyer at her Minehead boarding house was made during the summer and resulted in several pleasing views of the harbour, old cottages on the beach and similar subjects to which he turned again and again in later years.

At the turn of the century, Harry began for the first time to feel the full impact of competition from picture postcards which was to have a significant effect on his life and work. Introduced in Austria in 1881, postcards showing vignetted views of towns superscribed with the words 'Gruss Aus' (greetings from) soon became very popular

*Harry Frier, c.1900, aged 50.*

*Kate Frier, c.1900, aged 50.* A carte-de-visite taken by Arnold, London Studio, Taunton.

with tourists on the Continent. Some were printed in colour by chromo-lithography, but most were in monochrome. The British Post Office refused to permit the transmission of such postcards unless enclosed in an envelope. In 1894, however, the Post Office relented and opened the way to the expansion of the picture postcard industry. By 1900, in addition to national publishers of postcards, local photographers, stationers and newsagents published topographical picture postcards, tinted, printed and photographic, for sale in their own area. The proliferation of such postcards made life difficult for Harry. His topographic watercolours cost 5s or 7s.6d. (£10 or £15 today), at a time when picture postcards sold for a halfpenny or 1d (8p or 15p today) each. In order to be competitive, Harry had to sell more or produce them more cheaply. There were several ways in which the painting process could be accelerated. One was by using pen and ink instead of watercolour washes for areas of shadow detail, such as tiled roofs. Another was to paint foliage with a sponge instead of a brush. This technique is not easy, for the dampness of the paper and the quantity of paint on the sponge must be just right, but when well done it is quick and effective, for when the first application has dried, subsequent applications of different tints give the foliage sparkle and shading. When, as was sometimes the case, it was less skilfully applied the result resembled a colour production printed out of register which is disturbing to look at.

Another way of speeding the process was to paint highlights with Chinese white instead of leaving the white paper to show through, but since watercolour painting is perhaps as much concerned with what is left out as with what is applied to the paper, highlights produced by this means lack life and sparkle. In spite of ingenuity, artifice and increased production, Harry's income fell sharply after 1900. In his desperate struggle to sell his drawings Harry frequented Taunton's public houses, where he hawked them to anyone who would buy. Before offering drawings for sale, Harry usually mounted each on a large sheet of cheap white thick card with adhesive applied to the whole of the reverse of the drawing. He ruled a single Indian ink line on the mount about 6mm away from the edge of the picture and pencilled the title of the drawing at the upper edge of the reverse of the mount. As his mounts have often been cut down the titles are not always present. Occasionally he wrote the title in pencil on the reverse of the drawing itself.

In 1901 he painted a 50 x 75cm watercolour of North Hill at Minehead seen from the Warren, with donkeys and bathing machines on the beach in the foreground. Perhaps it was painted in reply to the post-card menace, the creation of something which the opposition could never match, a gamble, for it took a long time and commanded a high price. One version of it was sold, but another hung in Vickery's shop window for months until it was quite faded by the sun. It was perhaps for the same reason that in 1903 he painted a large view of the Cross Keys Inn on the Minehead Road, near Norton Fitzwarren.

Shortage of money led to a further deterioration in relations with Kate. Their marriage became one of fierce recrimination by both, followed by long periods of moody silence. For the next few years their lives settled into a dull routine, and there is little doubt that they were both suffering from stress. Harry could still seek solace from the act of painting: all Kate had were her geraniums and her cat. Harry felt himself degraded by the process of trying to sell his work, hawking it round the pubs, reducing the price until a buyer was found. Sometimes, after making a sale he stayed on, enjoying the company of shopkeepers and other tradesmen, but he contributed little to their conversation. Although intelligent and educated, Harry took little interest in politics, religion or contemporary affairs. He was a good listener, but a poor talker; a man of many acquaintances but very few friends. His juvenile sense of fun could sometimes be put to good use. There lived next to the Convent a retired doctor called Lyddon whose coachman was mixed up in a Saturday-night brawl, during which he got a black eye. As he was due to drive the

doctor to church on the following morning he was afraid of what his employer might say about his eye. He met Harry and asked for help. Harry took him home, and, mixing oil colour with zinc ointment he was able to disguise the bruise and all was well.

Gradually he began to drink too much, not noticeably so at first, but as the years passed his drinking increased, as did the tension with Kate. She despised him for his laziness, for wasting money on drink, for his failure to sell his work. Harry retorted, with justification, that Kate was ugly, avaricious, and a miserable slattern, for that is what she was fast becoming.

In the three years after 1902 the number of Harry's recorded paint-ings fell considerably. Whereas he had painted about 120 in 1901, production fell to about 45 in 1902, and to 60 in 1903, 1904 and 1905. Thus it would seem that only Tite's commissions, not included in these figures, were saving Harry from penury. A photograph taken of Harry at about this time by William Crockett is annotated in Harry's hand: 'The President of the Taunton Band of Hope Temperance League' followed by his 'spectacles' signature. Regrettably, the occasion for the photograph is unknown.

The next few years saw a further decline in the quality of his work, his standard of living and his home life. Kate often settled her trades-men's accounts with pictures, so short was she kept of money. Reed & Giles, the fishmongers near the station, are said to have collected more than two dozen of his pictures by this means. Nevertheless, Harry still insisted on maintaining middle-class standards; the Friers were said to be the only household in Greenbrook Terrace who regularly ate their main meal in the evening rather than at midday. Theirs was the only house with a brass plate beside the front door with their name engraved on it; although customary in Scotland, it was unusual in Greenbrook Terrace. Harry usually left the house at about noon, neatly dressed in a tweed suit with brightly coloured waistcoat decorated with a gold 'Albert' watch chain. He put on a pair of starched linen cuffs fastened to his shirt sleeves with press studs, on his head a well-brushed bowler. His beard at this period of his life was cut to a goatee shape with waxed moustache points, although later he reverted to the full beard which he had worn since early manhood. He turned out of Greenbrook Terrace, into Wood Street, and walked with soldierly bearing up Bridge Street and on into North Street where, near its junction with Fore Street, he would turn into George Scarlett's. This was not an ordinary public house, but a more superior drinking establishment which catered for tradesmen and other middle-class people. By 1905 he did not see too well with his one good eye in the gloom of Scarlett's, and so in order to be served he banged on the floor with his cane and shouted his order to the barmaid. He became impatient if he was not served at once. After an hour or so in the company of people like Wickenden, the restaurant proprietor, Turner who owned the furniture shop in Billet Street, or Sibley, the tailor of Cheapside, he would return home for lunch. Passers by, seeing him walking down North Street on his way home could be forgiven for thinking him intoxicated, an impression that was heightened by the fixed stare of his damaged right eye. As one acquaintance put it: 'He was never intoxicated, but always pleasantly saturated.'

In the summer of 1905 the Friers managed a few days' holiday at Newquay, possibly in the company of the Crocketts. On an excursion Harry made a sketch of Lanverne church near St Mawgan. Also from this stay came two seascapes. One is a view from the cliff top looking down across a cove to cliffs on the far side; a solitary figure walks purposefully across the broad sandy beach below. The other, a dramatic view of a mass of jagged rock thrusting through the centre of the scene, has been much affected by damp. On the reverse of the mount was written, either by Kate Frier or May Crockett, 'By the summer sea, end of headland, Newquay'.

As the popularity of picture postcards increased, so Harry's sales waned. It is possible that he was beginning to fall behind with the rent; certainly Kate was struggling to make ends meet and payment of bills in kind became more frequent. It seems that Kate was beginning to be afraid of Harry and often took pictures for this purpose while he was out, but the recompense she received was less than their worth. From all this Harry remained aloof; he expected her to attend to household debts, while he stayed upstairs painting. Gradually, his appearances at the dining table became more infrequent as he reckoned to be too busy to eat and demanded that his meals be brought up to him. Soon he lived permanently on the first floor, while Kate lived and slept downstairs, where her chief occupation seems to have been the cultivation of her geraniums which grew in profusion on every ground floor window sill. She kept a few fowls in the back garden, and if they ventured through the open door of the kitchen looking for food, they often stayed until nightfall enjoying the cool summer shade.

Sales were still falling and prices had to be further reduced. A 17.5 x 27.5cm watercolour drawing was now sold for between 2s.6d. and 5s (£7.50 to £15 today), and to maintain income productivity had to be increased further. The pen was already being used for tile shadows, and, with white, for highlights. Now the use of body-colour also began to increase. Much of the luminosity and sparkle of water-colours derives from the transparency of the medium through which the white paper may still be seen. The application of washes of watercolour demands thought, care and considerable self-discipline if the transparency is not to be lost and the drawing become clouded and muddy. The process is time-consuming and demands fine judgement of the paper's dampness or otherwise, depending on the humidity of the weather and the time of year. Some washes must be laid while the paper is wet, some while it is merely damp, and some dragged onto dry paper with a nearly dry brush. Body-colour or gouache, which is essentially watercolour mixed with Chinese white to render it opaque, may be applied in layers, by an additive process similar to oil painting. It is easier and quicker to apply, as, unlike oil pigments, body-colour dries quickly. These were the advantages which Harry now sought to exploit; but the gains were not all posi-tive. Carelessly handled, body-colour pigments applied using a watercolour technique result in a degrading of the hues, so that the finished painting is dull and lifeless. Picture postcards were indeed beginning to destroy him.

As if to rub salt into his wounds, some of his watercolour drawings were used for making printed picture postcards without his signa-ture appearing on them. Amongst them was one of the White Hart Inn, showing the south side of Fore Street, which Harry had painted for Charles Tite, and another of old shops in Bridge Street, the 'origi-nals' of which were in each case signed by Harry. In addition he is reputed to have produced for Barnicotts a set of Taunton scenes which were issued in postcard form. There is an unsupported tradi-tion that he prepared drawings for vulgar seaside comic postcards. One is supposed to have shown a customs officer examining the opened suitcase of a lady traveller. 'Madam,' he is saying, 'I believe you have a false bottom.' The sequel was on the reverse of the picture and is supposed to have shown the woman bending over with skirts raised, saying, 'Young man, you can see it's not false.'

In 1908 Harry was approached for tuition in painting by a young man of eighteen, Wilfrid Hawkins, who lived in East Reach, Taunton. From the age of fifteen, Hawkins had attended the School of Art, then housed in the Victoria Rooms overlooking the Parade. Tiring of the stereotyped tuition that he was receiving there, and being an admirer of Frier's style, Hawkins asked his father to see if Harry would take him as a pupil. At first Harry refused, but after a few weeks he reluctantly agreed to 'see how the boy shaped'. So began four years of weekly visits by the young man at a fee of 5s (£15) a visit. The lessons were held on Thursday afternoons in Harry's studio in the front bedroom of 15 Greenbrook Terrace, and consisted principally of Hawkins copying Harry's pictures to learn the technique.

The Assize Fair, painted in 1909, was commissioned by Charles Tite and was intended to illustrate the scene on Castle Green during the fair of 1854. Against a backdrop of the Winchester Hotel, the castle and two large poplars, Harry has depicted all the stalls and sideshows which formed the fair. All is bustle and activity, crowded with life. Tite wanted even more figures to be added, but Harry declined. He had been occupied with the picture for two or three weeks and was tired of it, whereupon Tite said, 'Put in another pound's worth of people and I will take it.' Harry agreed, but it was Hawkins who put them in.

In spite of all, Harry enjoyed painting. A few pictures have been seen bearing dedications on the reverse, for they were given as presents to friends. One to Crockett, the photographer, was a small monochrome showing a small sailing vessel tied up at the quay at Minehead, balanced by Conygar Tower in the distance. Another watercolour of Wroxham Broad in Norfolk was a birthday present to Mrs Crockett and was inscribed: 'To May Crockett from the old master, the celebrated...' and there follows the symbol of the spectacles with one eye blacked out. A view of Rose Cottage, Clovelly, painted in 1915 was inscribed: 'To Archie Smith and Maggie Meek on their wedding, April 5th 1915, with kind wishes for their

*Harry Frier, c.1908.* Taken by W A Crockett, Bath Place, Taunton and annotated by Harry Frier.

future happiness and prosperity, from the painter, Harry Frier, Taunton'.

At home relations with Kate were not so cordial. He treated her with a certain contempt, expecting her to be always at his beck and call, to fetch his beer, for example, if he were too busy to go out. Sometimes she would be dispatched to obtain more materials on credit from

*Kate Frier at the gate of 15 Greenbrook Terrace, Taunton, c.1908.* The first-floor window was that of Harry's workroom.

Vickery. Harry would not do this for himself; it was not seemly for the head of the household to haggle with tradesmen. It was Kate's duty to move Harry's worktable and place another near it for young Hawkins to use, so that both could share the light from the window. One day, this task completed, Kate asked, 'What do you want me to do now, Harry?' 'Shift!' he replied. She left without a word. Harry often had a pint mug of beer on his worktable from which he occasionally took a sip; he dipped his brush into it too, sometimes. One day he picked up the mug, but put it down with a grunt. 'The old bitch has drunk my beer,' he said, for Kate was also fond of a drink. She also had to pick up his brush if he dropped it; he called down to her to come and pick it up, and she had to trudge upstairs to do it. If she was too slow he would call again, adding, 'Where the bloody hell are you?' so that half the street could hear.

In Hare's jewellery shop on Taunton's Parade the employees were provided with a hot midday meal in the workshop behind the shop, prepared by Mrs Hare. At Christmas and sometimes on other occasions, there would be a special lunch, and Harry was asked to design small menu and place cards for table decoration. They were illustrated with watercolour vignettes. On occasion he was taken by Mr Hare in his car to Minehead: a Swift, this is reputed to have been one of the first cars in Taunton. They visited Mrs Hare's parents' farm at the Warren, on part of which the golf course was built, and Harry painted a view of the links in 1909 with Mrs Hare standing by the tee. In the background are the bell tents of the Territorials who used the beach at the Warren as a rifle range.

In 1911 Harry took as a second pupil Mabel Crockett, the photographer's daughter, then aged thirteen. This must have been a charitable act on Crockett's part, for Mabel had little aptitude for painting. There followed more pupils, amongst them the Misses Esdaile of Cothelstone House, and Arthur Woodrow, whose lessons began in 1911. Their tuition fees contributed much to Harry's income at a time when he was barely able to sell a picture. Woodrow, like Hawkins and Mabel Crockett, came to Harry's house for tuition, but as far as the Esdailes were concerned, Harry travelled out to Cothelstone, about 6 miles from Taunton, on Hank's horse bus. The fare was 3d (about 50p today) single.

Kate and Harry were now quarrelling so much that their private lives became public property. Harry's drinking increased to such an extent that, on his return from the pub he sometimes blundered into the wrong house in Greenbrook Terrace. Bewildered, he looked

*Harry Frier with sketchbook.* Harry, wearing a flat cap, with a group on a horse bus outside the Parade Hotel, North Street, Taunton, c.1912: a detail from a larger photograph.

round the living room and muttered, 'Where the hell am I?' before shambling out again. Kate, dressed always in black and her hair was now quite grey, withdrew from society. Occasionally, when Harry managed to earn more than a bare living wage there would be a brief rapprochement. At such times they would go for a drink together and would return, both 'pleasantly saturated'. Sometimes after he came home Harry opened his workroom window, and calling to the street urchins, threw coppers into the street for them. When the bickering and recrimination resumed next day, Harry struck Kate and she would retreat to a neighbour's house for solace and feminine company. But not all their quarrels were serious. On occasion Kate would say to Harry, 'Go to hell!', to which he would retort, 'I shall have to if I want to see you again!' It is said that during one of their quarrels Harry slashed his oil portrait of Kate with a knife. Certainly there is a significant scratch on the portrait's face.

In an attempt further to increase productivity, Harry resorted to the batch production of pictures. An imperial sheet of paper was subdivided into eight rectangles, each 17.5 x 27.5cm, and the picture to be painted was pricked through or traced onto each rectangle in turn and redrawn eight times. Each was then rapidly painted in bodycolour, each tint being applied to all the drawings in turn, until eight identical drawings were complete. So desperate was he to go on turning out work that Harry felt compelled to work on into the night by the light of the gas globe on the wall. His health began to suffer, from poor food, too much drink and long hours of work. Kate too was not in good health. In 1912 they were both sixty-three years old. After Christmas Kate caught a severe chill: Harry is alleged to have refused to feed her chickens so she staggered out into the garden to look after them in the freezing January weather. She caught bronchitis and within a week was dead.

Harry suddenly realised the extent of his loss and was inconsolable. He paid for the insertion of an announcement of her death in the *County Gazette,* and after her funeral ordered the customary black-edged cards, with embossed silver lilies of the valley on the front, with the words: 'In loving memory of Kezia Catharine (Kate) the dear wife of Harry Frier, died 31st January 1913, aged 63, buried at Creech St Michael, 6th February 1913'. Alone for the first time for over thirty years, Harry was heartbroken. Whatever may have been their differences, their quarrels, their idiosyncratic life together, Harry realised how much he had loved her. It is said that Kate had taken out an assurance policy on Harry's life. However little money they had, she had always managed to keep the weekly premiums paid, but to prevent Harry from finding the policy and perhaps cashing it in, Kate hid it under the carpet. As he knew nothing of it, the premiums remained unpaid after her death, and the policy lapsed.

*Harry Frier, c.1912.*

Harry had little idea of how to look after himself. He survived with the help of friends and neighbours, but above all with the help of Kate's niece Lottie, who had run away from home in 1900 to be married in Cardiff to a bricklayer, George Brass. Now they were back in Taunton, living round the corner at 28 Portland Street. In spite of Lottie's help, Harry was completely demoralised. Street urchins came and went in and out of the house, almost the only visitors Harry had. He liked them and made use of them, sending them to Vickery's for colour, to Holt's or Gillards for snuff, and not infrequently to Scarlett's with a picture and a request for a bottle of whisky. Scarlett usually obliged. They boiled glue in the kitchen for Harry to mount his pictures ready for sale, and occasionally, for a dare, they would take a sip of his beer or look inside his workroom cupboard to see the drawings of nudes rumoured to be there. There were none, but Harry shouted at them just the same, worried lest they should disorganise his stacks of numbered sketches.

Friends, anxious to support him, commissioned from him paintings that perhaps sometimes they really did not want. Clode the fishmonger in East Street asked Harry to paint a view of his shop. Harry set up his board in the yard of the pub opposite and began work. After an hour or so he went in and asked Clode for something on account. This he drank at the pub, and went home. When he came the next day to continue the picture, Harry gave Clode another watercolour in return for the advance, and continued working on the view of the shop. After an hour or so, he went in and asked for something on account… Clode received several pictures as a result, but never the view of his shop that he had asked for.

In 1911 Harry was so busy with pupils that he produced no more than about 20 watercolour drawings, and in 1912, fewer than that. After Kate's death he gave no more tuition. He withdrew from the world and from the company of friends to such an extent that no one knew quite what had become of him. With the exception of his short-lived excursion into monochromes, no significant development or innovation in his work is evident until after Kate's death. Thereafter, for reasons which may have been fortuitous, perhaps as a result of finding that body-colour was cheaper and easier to manage than watercolour or of a deterioration of his sight, Harry began to use bold blocks of colour in sombre hues. His work assumed an entirely different character. Eerie, enigmatic and almost nightmarish paintings of landscapes, these works have an unearthly quality. Between 1914 and 1919, the views of Taunton or Minehead, which he had painted several times before, look as if they were the work of a different man. Viewed in isolation rather than as historical documents, they have a kind of morbid fascination, the work of someone who was profoundly unhappy. At the time they were produced they were probably unsaleable, but now some of these are among the more interesting and original of his works. It is instructive, for example, to compare the highly finished version of North Hill and the cottage on the beach at Minehead, painted in 1900, with the same view painted in 1917; the two are poles apart, but both, although very different in their approach, have merit.

He no longer sketched in the open air, indeed he hardly went out at all, and when he did, it was to walk slowly, leaning heavily on his stick, the few hundred yards to the Black Horse or the Myrtle. Instead he painted in his new style popular subjects such as North Hill at Minehead, from his old sketches, but he also copied extensively commercial picture postcards, views of Clovelly, Dartmoor and Alphington, the originals of which had been painted by Sidney Endacott of Exeter, G H Jenkins or E D Percival. By the end of 1914 he was so impoverished and ill that Lottie took pity on him and persuaded her husband to allow her to take Harry into their house as a lodger. Harry was sixty-five years old, and aging rapidly, but the compulsion to paint was undiminished.

Two years later, Harry's presence as a lodger in the Brass household was becoming intolerable. The house in which their young family was growing up was small. The children needed separate rooms. Not only was Harry taking this much needed space for his bed and his watercolour board, but he was untidy, irreligious and given to occasional bouts of drunkenness and swearing, which was not acceptable in a strongly Chapel household. He disrupted the family routine with his demands for dinner at night, he was dirty and it is likely that there were already signs of the onset of senility, so that he was becoming even more difficult to live with. George Brass's opportunity of ejecting this cuckoo from the nest came in the spring of 1917, when his eldest son Samuel found a job at Woolwich Arsenal near the home of Frances Powell, his aunt. It was arranged that he should go to lodge with her. The whole family went to see him safely settled in, but it was not possible to take Harry as well and so it was that he entered the Poor Law Institution for the first time on 7 April 1917.

The Poor Law Institution, always known as the workhouse, was a refuge of last resort, a place to be avoided at all costs. Established in the 1830s as a means of relieving distress amongst the indigent at minimum cost to the ratepayers, workhouses quickly became a byword for inhumanity and privation. Wives were separated from husbands, children from parents, but all were expected to work long hours at menial tasks in return for inadequate food and cold comfort. The administration of the Poor Law was in the hands of a Board of Guardians who appointed the Master of the workhouse, and the Matron, often the master's wife. Together they were responsible for the enforcement of the strict rules which governed the lives of the unfortunate inmates for life in the workhouse was not intended to be pleasant. Workhouses were meant to deter, not attract. So it was that few personal possessions were permitted, and all privacy was denied to the inmates who lived, worked, ate and slept in common, the women and children on one side of the building, the men on the other.

In 1917 the Master of Taunton's workhouse was Thomas Gerry and his wife was Matron. They had charge of the 410 inmates, most of whom were capable of working at cooking, cleaning or gardening. Those who were too old or feeble to work could do nothing: as often as not they were bedridden, and were provided with beds with iron cot sides to prevent them from falling out. If they became too troublesome their hands were sometimes tied to the bedhead to control them. Constructed in 1837, just to the east of South Street the Taunton Workhouse was cold, inhospitable and badly lit, and in the dark days of winter was depressing beyond belief. Nevertheless, the inmates were not prisoners, and could be taken away by relatives or discharge themselves at any time if their financial circumstances improved. It is hardly surprising that if he believed he had grounds for complaint while living with George and Lottie Brass, Harry was horrified at conditions in the workhouse. He was utterly miserable and after six weeks finally persuaded Lottie to take him back to Portland Street.

The record of Harry's first admission to the workhouse indicates that he was suffering from gout. There is little doubt that in addition to symptoms of gout, Harry was perhaps already beginning to suffer from dementia. After six months as their lodger again in the summer and autumn of 1917, Harry was once more admitted to the workhouse on Christmas Day of that year. The reason is not known, but on admission he was described as 'feeble', perhaps indicating a phase of confusion and disorientation. However, on 25 January 1918, he discharged himself, but a week later he was re-admitted, and once more his condition on entry was described as 'feeble'. He remained there for ten weeks until 5 March, when he discharged himself. Perhaps there was some remission of his condition, for he went to stay for a month at Polly's boarding house at Glenmore Road, Minehead, but the impending arrival of the summer visitors at Easter meant that Harry had to leave and find somewhere else to live.

In April he wrote to Lottie's mother, Charlotte, who since 1894 had been living-in housekeeper to Alderman Spiller in Taunton. In his letter, Harry said that he had heard from Lottie that 'Mr Spiller had one or two houses to let behind Scott's the jewellers,' in the area of the Old Pig Market between High Street and Paul Street. 'I have to get back to Taunton presently to paint a large portrait of a mayor in his civic robes for Mr Chaffin… and I must have somewhere to go.' Chaffin was a photographer with premises next to Claridge's London Hotel, now Waterstone's bookshop; it is likely the painting work Harry mentioned involved either the tinting of a photograph, or preparing a mayoral portrait copied from one of Chaffin's photographs.

Presumably the rent of Spiller's houses was more than Harry could afford, for later in the year he lodged in the District Nurse's house in Paul Street. Here he subsisted on the 7s (£18) a week pension from Charles Tite and from sales of his work, poor though this had by now become. Some new pictures from this period well illustrate the despair that was beginning to overtake him. They depict strange views of Dartmoor or the Scottish Highlands. Lonely and devoid of human figures, they have a weird almost nightmarish quality: landscapes of unearthly grandeur, dark, with pink or yellow skies and cold, silent, lonely lochs. Whatever may have been his state of mind when he painted these landscapes, they are nevertheless, as was his custom, signed and carefully dated. His last signed and dated work was painted in 1919, a watercolour of Sandhill Park lake at Bishop's Lydeard, showing the ornamental bridge dividing the picture in two horizontally against a background of trees. In the foreground on the lake are two figures in a skiff. The first version of this picture had been painted 'from nature' in 1896, but the 1919 version is based on a pencil sketch dated 1898. The cheap colours used have now become blue, but otherwise it is not an unsatisfactory work for its date.

Harry was now sixty-nine, a sad wreck of a man: his hair was now quite white, his tall shoulders stooped, his one eye losing its vigour. He was dressed in threadbare clothes, many of which were sent to him by his sister Mary from Leeds. His beard was matted with Wilson's SP snuff to which he was addicted. Although nominally independent and paying his way, he could not have managed without Tite's pension, which was almost his only income at this time. As the year turned to autumn, and the war ended, his work began to lose touch with any semblance of reality. It became ever more childlike in its execution, and was no longer dated, and sometimes unsigned. For the first time in his life Harry could not sell a single picture; he was no longer capable of earning a living.

In March 1919, he was evicted from his lodgings in Paul Street and was once more taken to the workhouse. As he said in a letter written from Taunton Union Infirmary to Charlotte on 31 March:

*By the address you will see where I am again… I was brought here by two policemen who found me wandering about the street at one o'clock in the morning looking about for a bed. I had walked the streets nearly all the night before, nowhere to sleep, cold and miserable…*

Clearly his lack of awareness was not yet total, for between April and August 1919 he wrote several letters to Charlotte describing his pathetic state:

*It is most uncomfortable here; got to get out of bed at five in the morning and the nurses and wardsmen are very cruel.*

He was obsessed with time and pleaded to have his watch which he thought Lottie's son Cecil had taken for repair, and to pay for which Harry had given Cecil 22s (£23 today) worth of pictures. All he had to look forward to was his old age pension which he would receive after 2 May 1919.

By this time, Charlotte was becoming sick and tired of Harry's complaints, and she must have said as much to him during a visit in March 1919. This resulted in some mutual recrimination and a suggestion by Charlotte that Harry had not loved Kate and had been cruel to her during her lifetime – a suggestion which perhaps had some truth in it. When Harry wrote to her in April he whined pathetically:

*You cannot miss Kate as I do: I never was unkind to Kate: all the time she lived with me she was good to me, and so was I to her. My mother and sisters were dead against my marrying her, but afterwards they were all very good to her.*

Later in April he wrote to Charlotte, and reiterated his desire to leave. To the end of his life his compulsion to paint was undiminished. He asked her for the needles 'on my late mantelpiece in a tin box' and underneath appended a drawing of a 7.5cm long pin, which he used for pricking through his sketches when he wanted to paint from them:

*At present of course, I am making nothing… As for my things in Paul Street, I shall be pleased if you could put them aside for me till I come out of here.*

Again he refers to 'getting out after 2nd May to draw the pension they are going to give me' and to his seventieth birthday:

*Mr Tite is coming to see me on 2nd May. Last year he brought me some tea, a big cake and some other things when I invited four or five in the room to tea and cake. I am dreadfully miserable just now… We got to be in bed at six, and up at five mornings.*

He was still not out of the workhouse by his birthday, still without his watch and still desperate to leave, repeating endlessly his request for his 'painting things and my clothes, dirty, which I left in a drawer in my old room when I left Paul Street', the pins again, and his photos of his family. He could be perverse too, remarking in May, a few days later, that:

*I ought to be out this fine weather to get stronger. All the inmates here are to be driven out next Tuesday for a holiday. I will not go.*

In July he wrote:

*I am confined entirely to bed, not allowed to get up or get out in the fresh air… The master will not allow me out in my stockings, and I have no boots to put on. I can never get any better: lying in bed every day like this only makes me weaker. That is the reason I must have my slippers…*

Workhouse conditions preyed on his mind. On 8 August 1919 he wrote:

*My whole life is ruined, and today I am left nearly alone as all here are off for a drive given by the Guardians, it is a most unhappy life for me, as all the men here are quarrelsome and so greedy… Six men have died in my ward since I came into it, out of seven who were in it including myself. It makes a man so awfully depressed.*

His frame of mind was understandable.

*Letter dated 21 July 1919, to Charlotte Brass written by Harry Frier.*

He wrote no more letters after August 1919. His mind was disintegrating, his body becoming ever more feeble. A visitor who saw Harry at about this time described the pathetic figure in his iron cot, coughing and mumbling incomprehensibly, while his visitors, bored, stared round the room unable to communicate with him. Understandably their visits became less frequent and probably ceased altogether by the end of the year. Harry lived on, inert, his mind apparently devoid of any conscious thought, until he died, mind and body worn out, on Saturday 19 February 1921. His death certificate, witnessed by the Master of the workhouse, Thomas Gerry, gave as the cause of death 'senile decay', and as the place of death '9 Union Street, Taunton', concealing from the casual glance the fact that it was at the workhouse that Harry died.

Charles Tite, his friend and benefactor for more than twenty years, wrote the obituary that appeared in the *County Gazette* on 26 February 1921:

> *…Tauntonians of the future will owe Mr Frier a debt of gratitude for having preserved for them sketches of many of the old buildings in Taunton which have now been demolished. Others will thank him for delightful glimpses of favourite bits of scenery in the neighbourhood; and still others for the happy knack he had of easily delineating local characters or the nooks and corners of old Taunton… He was a remarkably clever copyist, and was often permitted to reproduce rare sketches of local interest, thus adding considerably to the value of many a collection.*

It is not clear whether Tite's patronage of Harry was intended to preserve in the public domain views of Taunton and elsewhere that Tite realised would one day be swept away, or to provide support for a worthy but unsuccessful painter. Harry's engagement by Tite to copy in watercolour prints and photographs already safely lodged in the Archaeological Society's private collection suggests that Tite was motivated by both these considerations. Tite emphasised the significance of the painter's legacy, yet it is only since the upsurge of interest in local history during the last thirty years or so that both Tite's patronage and Harry's work have been appreciated as a valuable contribution to the historical record of a Taunton that has since undergone significant change.

At his death, Harry was destitute, any possessions he once had were claimed by George and Lottie Brass. Some were sold, perhaps to pay his small debts, but there was no money for his burial. Harry's sister Mary sent £25 (£550) to George Brass to pay for the simple funeral, and so on 24 February 1921, he was buried in the churchyard at Creech St Michael. The day was cold, the wind blowing flurries of snowflakes into the bearers' faces as the plain elm coffin was lowered into the same grave in which Kate had been buried eight years before. The site of their grave is unknown. The only mourners were the Brass family whose daughter Margery remembers the day only for the fact that she was sick on the way home.

So ended the life of Harry Frier. Like many others it began full of aspiration and hope, but as aspiration was first snuffed out by the chill wind of economic forces and hope dwindled almost to nothing, perseverance alone remained. It is difficult to imagine what he could have done if he had not become a painter. His life had been 'directed' from the age of six; his temperament and upbringing would probably have made him unsuited to working as a bank clerk, or in one of the many cloth merchants' premises in Lawnmarket. Perhaps he should have continued as drawing teacher, a calling that he discovered as a young man but only rediscovered much later in life. It is possible that his early experience at George Watson's College and its sister institution had discouraged him from continuing in that field; besides, he was determined to make a name for himself as a portrait painter. In the early years of the twentieth century as the certainties of the Victorian era were displaced by misgiving and insecurity, Harry found it difficult to adapt. By the time of Kate's death in 1912 the world had passed him by. Nevertheless it is a tribute to his technical competence and to his modest demands, that he was able to support himself and his wife for so long. Compelled by upbringing and environment to paint, he could and wished to do nothing else; he lived, feckless as a man, immature as an artist, only dimly aware of the hard ways of the real world. Receiving little, he gave much. He left a legacy of which many more successful men may be envious, for his work has been taken to the far corners of the earth, to be cherished as a reminder of the places of Somerset and of the man who painted them.

# Epilogue

Maggie Eliza Frier, Harry's younger sister, who took over in October 1893 from her late father as teacher of drawing at George Watson's Ladies' College, was, it will be recalled, married to her second cousin, William Frier, in July 1897. They moved to Leeds where after some years, Maggie's sister Mary Frier joined them. Mary probably died in the late twenties and Maggie in about 1940. Jessie Frier stayed in Edinburgh, unmarried, and died in 1923. She is buried in her parents' grave in Dean Cemetery. Charles Tite, Harry's benefactor, died aged ninety-one on 16 May 1933 and is buried in St Mary's cemetery, Taunton. Kate's sister Charlotte died in February 1939, aged eighty-four, and her daughter Lottie Brass died, aged sixty-seven, in September 1944. They are both buried in the same plot in St Mary's cemetery, Taunton. George Brass became a builder, working from his home in Portland Street, Taunton, and died aged seventy-nine in May 1957.

*Norfolk: evening on Wroxham Broad, 1906.*
Watercolour, 12 x 17.8cm, signed and dated.

*A note on the reverse by Frier shows that this was a present to May Crockett, the photographer's wife. It was copied from a picture postcard.*

# Sources & Acknowledgements

That part of the foregoing account which deals with Harry Frier's forebears and his early life inevitably owes something to conjecture. The only surviving records are entries in parish registers, listings in Edinburgh trade directories, newspaper articles, decennial census returns and the archives of the Royal Scottish Academy and George Watson's College in Edinburgh. It may therefore be assumed that statements of fact have their origins in one or other of these sources the individual acknowledgement of which would require numerous footnotes.

For the account of his middle and later life, reliance has been chiefly placed on oral tradition (his written legacy comprises a handful of letters only) passed by Harry to his numerous acquaintances, who have in turn handed them on. Thus, with the exception of Registrars' records, rate books and records of the Poor Law Institution, this account owes almost everything to the recollection of those selfless people who have given generously of their time to pass on what they know or to ascertain what they do not.

In Somerset, they include:

The Council of Somerset Archaeological and Natural History Society.

D Bromwich, R J E Bush, J M Close, A Ellard, Mrs M Evason, A Fisher, D W Jeremiah, the late F Paul, the late Miss J D Peden, J Richards, Geoff Roberts, Selwood Antiques.

Somerset County Archivist, Somerset County Librarian, Somerset County Museums Officer, Somerset County Museum Education Service, Taunton Deane Borough Council.

In Scotland, they include: The Librarian, Edinburgh City Library.

The Secretary, Royal Scottish Academy.
The Registrar General, General Register Office, Edinburgh.
The Headmaster (then R W Young) George Watson's College, Edinburgh.
The Librarian (then H K Mackay) Baillie's Library, Glasgow.
J Bell.

In other parts of the country, information and assistance has been received from:
The late Wilfred Hawkins.
The Curator (then J R Rimmer), Warrington Municipal Museum and Art Gallery.
The Librarian, City of Leeds Public Library.

Among books and newspapers consulted and quoted from have been the following:
E Benezit *Dictionnaire des Peintres* Vol. 4, 1951, in which Harry Frier is listed as Harry Freer.
R J E Bush, *The Book of Taunton*, Chesham,1977.
R J E Bush, *Jeboult's Taunton*, Buckingham,1983.
J L Caw, *Scottish Painting Past & Present*, Edinburgh,1908.
Eric Linklater, *Edinburgh*, London,1960.
R L Stevenson, *Edinburgh: Picturesque Notes*, London,1889.
W D Mackay, *The Scottish School of Painting*, London,1906.
Martin Hardie, *John Pettie, RA, HRSA*, London, 1908, in which Pettie's sojourn with the Frier family and Harry Frier's visit to London with John Noble is described.

*The Scotsman.*
*Edinburgh Evening Dispatch.*
*Somerset County Gazette.*

*Landscape, possibly a view of Loch Tay from Finlarig, near Killin.*
Watercolour and body-colour, 29.2 x 46cm, by Robert Frier, Harry
Frier's father, signed and undated.

'A Private Examination', 1875.
Oil on canvas, 69.2 x 93.3cm, signed and dated.
Warrington Museum and Art Gallery.

*Portrait of the Gould family, near Obridge Lock, Lambrook Farm, Taunton, 1884.*
Oil on canvas, 1884, 60 x 91cm, signed and dated.

This painting was shown at the exhibition to raise money for the Taunton School of Art (then in Bath Place), held in the Great Hall of Taunton Castle for two weeks in October 1885, where, although it was awarded the silver medal for the best oil painting in the show, the newspaper critic merely observed that it was 'one of Frier's best efforts'. The flood prevention scheme of the 1960s resulted in the river being diverted 150 metres to the north, and the nearby Obridge lock was demolished as part of a new road scheme in the 1980s. In the same exhibition in 1885, Frier was awarded a bronze medal for the second best watercolour, the silver medal in that class going to Miss L Deane.

*Bathpool: cottage in Hyde Lane, c.1884.*
Watercolour, 10.8 x 15.2cm, signed with monogram but undated.

*House with walled garden, 1885.*
Watercolour, 26.7 x 36.8cm, signed and dated.

*Creech St Michael: main street looking south, 1885.*
Watercolour, 31.7 x 48.3, signed and dated.

*Farmhouse – girl with parasol, 1886 (detail).*
Watercolour, 37.5 x 53.3cm, signed and dated.

*Creech St Michael: canal looking west, 1887.*
Watercolour, 26.7 x 38.1cm, signed and dated.

*Bathpool: house on the north side of the crossroads, 1890.*
Watercolour, 36.8 x 60.1cm, signed and dated.

*Taunton: flood and fire Wood Street.*
Watercolour, 24 x 36.5cm, signed but undated.  TDBC.

*Bathpool: market garden in Hyde Lane, 1890.*
Watercolour, 33 x 48.3cm, signed and dated.

*Taunton: St John's church and French Weir from the north bank of the River Tone, 1890.*
Watercolour, 49.5 x 75.6cm, signed and dated in red.

H. Frier 1891.

*Taunton: Tone Bridge house from the south, 1891.*
*Watercolour, 20.3 x 29.2cm, signed and dated.*
*SANHS.*

*The house belonged to William Trood, manufacturer*
*of artificial fertiliser, whose son Henry was the well-*
*known deaf and dumb painter of dogs. Moored in*
*front of the house is the electrically powered launch*
*which was used in connection with Henry*
*Massingham's Electrical Exhibition held at his*
*firm's new Electric Works in St James' Street in*
*Taunton, in that year. Massingham owned a boot*
*and shoe shop in what is now Corporation Street*
*and had first lit the Parade by electricity in 1885,*
*one of the earlier examples of electric street lighting*
*in Britain.*

*Taunton: the town mill from the north bank of the River Tone, 1891.*
Watercolour,  18.4 x 26cm, signed and dated.   SANHS.

*Taunton: yard of the Four Alls Inn, looking west, 1892.*
Monochrome watercolour, 15.2 x 22.8cm, signed and dated.  SANHS.

*Taunton: Coal Orchard Wharf, 1892.*
Pen and ink and monochrome watercolour, 11.4 x 16.5cm,
signed with monogram and dated.

*Taunton: Staplegrove Road, looking east, 1892.*
Monochrome watercolour, 19 x 27.9cm, signed and dated. SANHS.

*Taunton: two shops in Bridge Street, 1892.*
Watercolour, 17.1 x 26.7cm, signed and dated. SANHS.

*Taunton: St James' Almshouses, looking west, 1892.*
Pen and ink, 14 x 11.4cm, signed and dated.

*'Taking stock'*, 1893.
Watercolour, 26.6 x 16.5cm, signed and dated.

*'Biting criticism', 1893.*
Pen and pencil on paper, 14 x 22.8cm, signed with monogram and dated.

*Harry was painting on land on the Quantocks and the ponies, curious as always, disturbed him, and compelled him to retreat. As the ponies damaged his canvas, umbrella and other materials, Harry sent an invoice to the Thrextons, who owned the land, for 5s. Payment was made, and this drawing was given by way of receipt. The title is written on the mount.*

*Ruishton: the Blackbrook Inn, 1893.*
Monochrome watercolour, 13.3 x 19cm, signed and dated.  TDBC.

*Taunton: Obridge Lock, Priory, looking south to Holy Trinity Church, 1894.*
Watercolour, 26 x 18.4cm, signed and dated.
SANHS.

*Charlotte Elizabeth Dyer, aged 18, 1895.*
Oil on canvas, 38.1 x 28cm, signed and dated.

*Taunton: footbridge over Obridge Lock, looking north, 1895.*
Pencil on paper, 12.7 x 17.8cm, unsigned but dated.

*Taunton: footbridge over Obridge Lock, looking north*, 1895.
Watercolour, 18.4 x 25.4cm, signed and dated.  SANHS.

*Taunton: Purchase's Yard, Wood Street.*
Pencil on paper, unsigned and undated.

*Bathpool: timber yard beside the Taunton and Bridgwater canal, 1895.*
Watercolour, 17.8 x 28cm, signed and dated.

*Creech St Michael: Ham Mill, 1897*.
Watercolour, 25.5 x 36.5cm, signed and dated.  TDBC.

*Taunton: interior of St James' Almshouses, 1896.*
Watercolour, 25.4 x 17.1cm, signed and dated.

*The drawing was commissioned by Charles Tite shortly before the almshouses were demolished in 1896. The timber frame of one of the dwellings has been re-erected in the courtyard of Taunton Castle Museum, and the external walls and roof have been restored to match the original. The drawing is one of only a handful of interiors that Frier is known to have painted.*

*Porlock Weir (?): cottage by the sea, 1897.*
Watercolour, 18.4 x 27.3cm, signed and dated.

*Taunton: Sugar Loaf Inn, Park Street.*
Watercolour, 20.3 x 128cm, signed with monogram but undated.
SANHS.

*A copy of a photograph taken by Edward Jeboult, c.1865.*

*Taunton: the lodge and school in South Road, later to become the Franciscan convent, before 1810.*
Watercolour, signed with monogram but undated, 16.3 x 25.4cm.  SANHS.

*Taunton: courtyard of St James' Street Almshouses, 1897.*
Watercolour, 17.1 x 26cm signed and dated.  SANHS.

*Taunton: old door, Portman House, 1898.* Watercolour, 25.4 x 19cm, signed and dated. SANHS.

"Hunting Bob"                    1898.

*'Hunting Bob', a strapper who followed hounds, 1898*
Watercolour, 17.8 x 12.7cm, signed with monogram and dated.
SANHS.

'Sweep', 1903.
Watercolour,  25.4 x 17.8cm, signed and dated.  SANHS.

'Billy Brewer', 1898.
Watercolour, 17.1 x 12.7cm, signed and dated. SANHS.

*Brewer (1817–90) was a pipe maker and grocer in Alfred Street, Taunton, who had a local reputation as a fortune-teller.*

*Taunton: panorama from the east, 1898.*
Watercolour, 50.1 x 73.7cm, signed and dated. TDBC.

*The scene was almost certainly drawn from the slope of Creechbarrow Hill, near to the old lane to Bathpool, then known as Roman Road, now Creechbarrow Road. From left to right in the picture the church towers are those of Holy Trinity, St George, St Mary, St John and St James. The buildings of Lambrook Farm are in front of the tower of St James' Church, and the Wellington Monument is just visible on the skyline in the centre of the view.*

*Taunton: the New Inn, Wilton, 1898.*
Watercolour, 23.5 x 31.1cm, signed and dated.  SANHS.

*This is now the Vivary Arms.*

*Taunton: the Four Alls Inn.*
Watercolour, 24.1 x 34.3cm, signed but undated. SANHS.

*The name originated from a seventeenth-century manuscript in the Ashmolean Museum, which stated that 'I (the king) rule all. I (the priest) pray for all: I (the soldier) fight for all, and I (the yeoman) pay for all.' The drawing shows the building before Corporation Street was constructed in 1894, and before the Four Alls itself was rebuilt. Perhaps the figure, admired only by a dog, was a fanciful self-portrait.*

*Taunton: Crown and Sceptre, Station Road.*
Watercolour, 19 x 26cm, signed but undated. SANHS.

*Minehead: view from the quay looking east, Conygar Tower in the distance, 1899.*
Watercolour,  24.1 x 44.5cm, signed and dated.

*Cottage on North Hill, Minehead, 1899.*
Watercolour, 16.2 x 26cm, signed and dated.

'Tom Locke, aged 90', 1899.
Watercolour, 20.3 x 15.2cm, signed with monogram and dated.  SANHS.

*Locke was the last 'potwalloper', the term for a someone who lived before 1832 within the old Borough of Taunton and who, until disenfranchised by the Reform Act of 1832, was entitled to vote in parliamentary elections.  Those already so enfranchised retained the right for life.*

*Taunton: coat of arms over the door of Gray's almshouses, 1899.*
Watercolour and body-colour, 26 x 20.3cm, signed and dated. SANHS.

*Norton Fitzwarren: old cottage, 1899.*
Watercolour, 17.8 x 25.4cm, signed and dated.  SANHS.

*The cottage has been demolished.*

*Taunton: cottages on the north side of Shuttern.*
Watercolour, undated, c.1899.

*The cottages were demolished many years ago.*

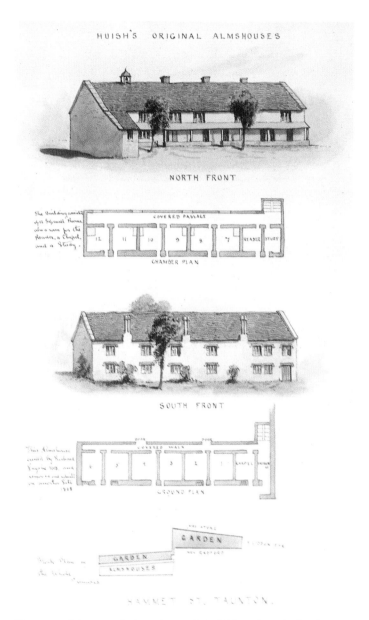

*Taunton: 'plans and elevations of Huish's original almshouses erected in Great Magdalene Lane 1625, demolished 1868'.*
*Watercolour with ink annotations, 31.1 x 22.2cm, undated.*
*SANHS.*

*Footbridge at Tower Lane, Taunton, 1899.*
Watercolour, 18.0 x 26.2cm, signed and dated.

*Minehead: cottage on the north side of Quay Street and North Hill, 1900.*
Watercolour, 27.3 x 34.3cm, signed and dated.   TDBC.

*An elaborately finished picture, possibly intended for exhibition: the cottage was demolished c.1908.*

*Minehead: cottage on the north side of Quay Street.*
Pencil on tracing paper, 12.7 x 22.9cm, unsigned and undated.

*Minehead: cottage on the north side of Quay Street, 1901.*
Monochrome watercolour, 18.4 x 28cm, signed and dated.

*Taunton: view of the town from Cotlake Hill (detail), 1901.*
Watercolour, 52 x 73.7cm, signed and dated.

*'Girl with a goose in a basket'*, 1901.
Watercolour, 26.7 x 18.4cm, signed
and dated.

*Nether Stowey: 'Billy Knight, broom squire', 1902.*
Watercolour, 17.8 x 26.7cm, signed and dated.  SANHS.

*The broom squire sold besoms which he made from materials gathered from Nether Stowey common.  The background is the courtyard of Taunton Castle.*

"Green Watercreeses"

H. Frier
1903.

*Taunton: 'green watercress', 1903.* Watercolour, 26.7 x 17.8cm, signed and dated. SANHS.

*Taunton: itinerant glazier with 'frail',*
*1903.*
Watercolour, 26.7 x 17.8cm, signed
and dated. SANHS.

"Milk Oh"

H. Frier.
1903

*Taunton: 'Milk oh!', 1903.*
Watercolour, 25.4 x 17.8cm, signed and dated. SANHS.

*Taunton: 'Jimmy the tinker' (James Atkins, 1880).*
Watercolour, 17.8 x 25.4, signed but undated.  SANHS.

Joe. Frost. "Tanky"
Pedestrian
Taunton.

Harry Frier 1903.

*Taunton: 'Joe Frost, 'Tanky', pedestrian', 1903. Watercolour, 26.7 x 17.8cm, signed and dated. SANHS.*

*Long-distance walking races, descendants of Victorian 'wobbles', and marathon running races were popular at the beginning of the twentieth century.*

*Taunton: 'H Dawe, the original army grinder', 1903.*
*Watercolour, 25.4 x 17.8cm, signed and dated.  SANHS.*

*Taunton: Cann Street looking north east, 1903.*
Pen and ink, 17.8 x 26.7cm , signed and dated.  SANHS.

*Taunton: Priory Avenue and the entrance to the Cricket Ground, 1903.*
Pen and ink, 25.4 x 18.4cm, signed and dated.  SANHS.

*Bridgwater and Taunton Canal: 'The money boat'.*
*Watercolour, 17 x 25cm, signed with monogram but undated.  TDBC.*

*This is a portrayal of the annual inspection of the canal by the Conservators of the River Tone in the 1854.*

*Taunton: 'Court behind no. 50, Fore Street, 1903'.*
Pen and ink, 17.8 x 26.7cm, signed and dated.  SANHS.

*Taunton: 'at the back of 44 and 45, East Street, 1903'.*
Watercolour, 17.8 x 26cm, signed and dated.
SANHS.

*Taunton: entrance to the old town mills, 1903.
Pen and wash, 25.4 x 17.8cm, signed and
dated.  SANHS.*

*The first mill is thought to have been built on
the site in the thirteenth century, with water
taken to the wheel along the mill stream from
what was later known as French Weir.  By the
early twentieth century, Small's Town Mills
were of interest to local artists: Francis
Colthurst drew a fine sketch of the interior at
about the same time as Frier depicted the
entrance arch leading from Mill Lane.*

*Taunton: No. 1 Court, Paul Street, 1903.*
Pen and ink, 17.8 x 26.7cm, signed and dated.  SANHS.

*Taunton: No. 8 Court, High Street, 1903.*
Pen and ink, 17.8 x 26.7cm, signed and
dated. SANHS.

*Taunton. No. 5 Court, St James' Street, 1903.*
Pen and ink, 13.3 x 18.4cm, signed and dated.

*One of the series of 'Courts and Corners of Taunton' made for Charles Tite, this is a view of the residential court which was near to the entrance of the County Cricket Ground. Like many other market towns, Taunton had numerous narrow residential courts opening from the principal streets of the town.*

111

*Taunton: back of the King's Arms, North Town, 1903.*
Pen and ink, 25.4 x 17.8cm, signed and dated. SANHS.

*Taunton: old Cockpit Farm, 1903.*
Pen and ink, 14 x 19cm, signed and dated. SANHS.

*The farm, on the site of a cockpit, was at the rear of the Royal Ashton Hotel in Station Road.*

*Taunton: Ivy Cottage at the foot of Haines Hill [sic], 1903.*
Pen and ink, 25.4 x 17.8cm, signed and dated. SANHS.

*The view is from the junction of Trull Road with Compass Hill; part of the Eye Infirmary may be seen on the left. The cottage has been demolished.*

*Taunton: back of Cheapside, 1903.*
Pen and ink, 25.4 x 17.8cm, signed and dated.  SANHS.

*Taunton: the old West Somerset Brewery, 1903.*
Pen and ink, 17.8 x 26.7cm, signed and dated.  SANHS.

*The tower of St James' Church is on the left of the view.*

*Lydeard St Lawrence: a cottage, 1903.*
Watercolour, 27.3 x 18.4cm, signed and
dated.

*Norton Fitzwarren: the Cross Keys Inn looking west.*
Watercolour, 25.4 x 135.6cm, signed and dated.

*The turning to Minehead is just beyond the tall tree on the left.*

*Taunton: market stalls, 1904.*
Watercolour, 17.8 x 25.4cm, signed and dated.  SANHS.

*Taunton: '1840, oysters threepence a dozen'.*
Watercolour, 17.8 x 25.4cm, signed but undated. SANHS.

*The scene is outside the side entrance of the Winchester Arms on Castle Green.*

"Cockles, a penny a plate"

H. Frier 1904.

*Taunton: 'Cockles, a penny a plate', 1904. Watercolour, 25.4 x 17.8cm, signed and dated. SANHS.*

*Taunton: constable c. 1860.*
Watercolour, 26.7 x 17.8cm, signed but undated.  SANHS.

*Taunton: Jimmy Morse, postman, 1904. Watercolour, 25.4 x 17.8cm, signed and dated. SANHS.*

*Inscribed: 'One armed, 32 years in the GPO, rural postman, Taunton and Lyng.'*

"Old Bottles or Jars."
"Rags or Bones"

H. Frier 1904

*Taunton: 'Old bottles, jars, rags or bones', 1904.*
Watercolour, 17.8 x 25.4cm, signed and dated.  SANHS.

*Taunton: 'The Eye Infirmary, Compass Hill, 1816', 1905.*
Pen and wash, 16.5 x 22.2cm, signed and dated. SANHS.

*The infirmary was established in 1816 in a former turnpike gatekeeper's house by James Billet, a surgeon and occulist: the infirmary closed in 1904, but the building still stands, divided into two dwellings, but with altered doors and windows.*

*Taunton: St James' Church tower.*
Pen and wash, 31.1 x 21cm, signed with monogram but undated. SANHS.

*A note below the drawing indicates that this shows the tower before its rebuilding in 1874.*

*Footbridge over the river Tone, Priory Fields, Taunton, ca. 1906.*
Watercolour, 15.8 x 26.2cm, signed but undated.

*Taunton: part of the east side of North Street, 1907.*
*Watercolour, 19.0 x 27.9, signed and dated. SANHS.*

*On the extreme right is the Spread Eagle Inn, demolished in 1911 to make*
*way for the post office building.*

*Taunton: mill stream looking west showing Woodley's printing premises, 1907.*
Watercolour, 24.7 x 17.8cm, signed and dated. SANHS.

*Born in 1818, William Woodley, at the age of twenty-five, was appointed editor of the Somerset County Gazette, which had been founded in December 1836 by Edward Cox. A few years later Woodley bought Cox's share of the business and moved the printing of the paper to this newly built steam printing works at Castle Green. In 1965 the firm was sold to Berrow's of Worcester, and printing at the works ended in 1972. The building was demolished in 1985. The bridge carried Tower Street over the mill stream.*

*Taunton: the old town bridge from the south west, 1908.*
Watercolour, 20.3 x 29.8cm, signed and dated.

*The sketch on which this drawing was based was made in 1892, three years before the structure was replaced by the present bridge.*

*Taunton: footbridge over Obridge weir, 1908.*
Watercolour, body-colour and Chinese white, 22.8 x 43.2cm, signed
and dated. TDBC.

*Picture postcards of this view were on sale at that time.*

*Taunton: east side of North Street, c.1850.*
Watercolour, 19 x 30.5cm, unsigned and undated.

*Taunton: the old town bridge looking upstream, 1908.*
Watercolour, body-colour and Chinese white, 20.3 x 37.5cm, signed and dated.

*This was based on a sketch made in 1892.*

*Taunton: George Inn, North Town.*
Pencil on tracing paper, 20.3 x 28cm, unsigned and undated.

*Taunton: the George Inn, North Town, 1909, drawn 1892.*
Body-colour, pen and ink, 19 x 27.9cm, signed and dated.

*The building was demolished and replaced by the Lyceum Theatre in 1912. On the right of the picture are the rails of the ambitiously named 'Taunton and West Somerset Electric Railways and Tramways Company Ltd' which ran from Rowbarton to the east end of East Reach from 1901 until 1921. Attached to the lamp standard in the centre of the view there used to be a long ladder intended for householders to gain access to thatched roofs when they caught fire. Laverock Court now stands on the site.*

*Taunton: 'Assize Fair, 1854', 1909.*
Watercolour with body-colour, 52 x 175cm, signed and dated in
yellow. SANHS.

*Bridgwater: 'The quay, copy of a lithograph by J Chubb'.* *The original print dates from 1790.*
Monochrome watercolour heightened with white, 10.1 x
15.2cm, unsigned and undated. SANHS.

*Taunton: 'Former Grammar School, after an old print', 1912.*
Watercolour, 30.5 x 43.1cm, signed and dated.

*The sunken garden was formerly part of Taunton Castle moat on which Corporation Street was constructed in 1894.*

*Taunton: Paul Street, looking north, 1913.*
Watercolour, body-colour, pen and ink 25.4
x 17.1cm, signed and dated.   SANHS.

*House by the stream, near Mount Terrace, Taunton, 1913.*
Watercolour, 17.3 x 11.2cm, signed and dated.  SANHS.

*Canal walk near Obridge, Taunton, 1913.*
Watercolour and body colour, 11.6 x 18.0cm, signed and dated. TDBC

*Taunton: St George's RC church, 1916.*
Body-colour, 26 x 36.2cm, signed and dated.

*The sketch on which this drawing was based was made in 1888.*

# Index